WEISER ☿ CLASSICS

THE WEISER CLASSICS SERIES offers essential works from renowned

authors and spiritual teachers, foundational texts, as well as

introductory guides on an array of topics written by contemporary

authors representing the full range of subjects and genres that

have been part of Weiser Books' over sixty-year-long publishing

program—from divination and magick to alchemy

and occult philosophy. Each volume in the series will include

new material from its author or a contributor and other valuable

additions to the work whenever possible and will be printed and

produced using acid-free paper in a durable paperback binding.

SPIRITUAL CLEANSING

SPIRITUAL CLEANSING

A Handbook of Psychic Protection

DRAJA MICKAHARIC

Foreword by Lilith Dorsey

WEISER BOOKS

This edition first published in 2022 by Weiser Books, an imprint of
Red Wheel/Weiser, LLC
With offices at:
65 Parker Street, Suite 7
Newburyport, MA 01950
www.redwheelweiser.com

ISBN: 978-1-57863-728-7
Library of Congress Cataloging-in-Publication Data
available upon request.

Cover design by Kathryn Sky-Peck
Cover photograph by iStock

Printed in the United States of America
IBI
10 9   8 7 6 5 4 3 2 1

SERIES EDITORS
Mike Conlon, Production Director, Red Wheel/Weiser Books
Judika Illes, Editor-at-Large, Weiser Books
Peter Turner, Associate Publisher, Weiser Books

SERIES DESIGN
Kathryn Sky-Peck, Creative Director, Red Wheel/Weiser

To those who taught me
that I might learn

Table of Contents

Foreword

Spiritual Cleansing by Draja Mickaharic is a classic magickal text. When I began studying magick, witchcraft, hoodoo, and other spiritual systems over four decades ago, written resources were few and far between. It was before the age of the Internet and social media, and much knowledge was transmitted by word of mouth. There were a choice few bookstores, and even fewer library sources on these topics. In addition, let's just say most of the few available practitioners were unhelpful at best. That's being kind. Access to information was a challenge, a quest almost, and there was one thing almost everyone I spoke to agreed upon—that Spiritual Cleansing is a necessary addition to any library. Even though it was written in 1982, it's still relevant, and in many ways even more important today.

Over the years people from all walks of life and spiritual traditions have recommended this book to me, and I have suggested it in turn to countless others. It can be very useful no matter what your specific magickal practice. I've seen ceremonial magicians, conjure doctors, witches, and many others sing its praises. Spiritual Cleansing contains something for everyone.

Draja Mickaharic has created a book that covers all the basics and then some. It begins with cautions, what to do, and what not to do, no matter what your level of experience is with these techniques. While some might think this is limiting, it is in fact the one true prerequisite for lasting success. Just as in mundane life, people need to walk before they can run, and our spiritual journeys are no different. Everything in these pages has been tested and verified by the author and others. All too often I see new authors making up new spells or rituals to meet a deadline or populate their news feed, the same way a toddler plays in the sandbox and thinks they're creating something real. The result may be cute, but it is rarely effective. A dear friend of mine likes to say that, with this type of behavior, the best possible result is nothing.

This book also makes the upfront distinction that this text is for spiritual cleansing only. All matters of physical healing and cleansing should be done by a medical professional. There is a lot that magick can do, but it must work in conjunction with sound medical practice in these areas.

Cleansing is the most vital component of any practitioner's magick; it can be a truly dirty world we live in both physically and spiritually. A competent practitioner will be prepared with an arsenal of solutions for most every eventuality. *Spiritual Cleansing* does just this, offering a variety of means and methods to help combat whatever life throws at you. There are cleansings here for your body, your mind, your home, and your wider environment. Each one provides help for specific spiritual issues.

My favorite section involves eggs. The chapter on egg cleansing is something that is both basic and universal. The use of eggs in magick is truly sublime; they represent potential and transformation in many different cultures. Here Mickaharic goes into detail about how to make this magickal cleansing work effectively for you in just about every situation. Egg cleansing utilizes the power of absorption. This particular type of cleansing allows the practitioner to drain the negativity from a person, place, or thing and then dispose of the egg accordingly. This can be done as often as necessary.

It was an honor to be asked to write the foreword to this book that I respect so highly. I do not say that lightly; there are very few authors whom I value as highly as Draja Mickaharic. His important words are both eloquent and concise, telling us just exactly what we need to know.

I hope you get from this book what you need. It is full to the brim with helpful solutions, that myself, my friends, my students, and my teachers use often. Every time I open it I am reminded just what a supreme treasure trove of spiritual tactics is contained here. Practitioners of all levels will find much usefulness here. A large proportion of magic is, at its core, about balance, and the interplay between energy in the universe. *Spiritual Cleansing* is a book that will help you restore that delicate balance in yourself and your surroundings. Just like the soap you use to cleanse your body, I hope you use this book often.

—Lilith Dorsey, author of
Orishas, Goddesses, and Voodoo Queens

SPIRITUAL CLEANSING

Introduction

Readers may wonder why anyone would want to write a book about spiritual cleansing. "What is it, anyway?" they might ask. Spiritual cleansing is often the easiest way to rid yourself of unwanted negative energy. Everyone has met an individual at some time or another who seems to be surrounded with negativity. Perhaps you sense the person has a "grey" or "dark" feeling. After spending a few minutes in the company of this negative individual you may feel tired or drowsy. You may even feel grimy or dirty after being near this person or shaking hands with him.

Maybe you walk into a house or apartment and immediately feel a desire to leave. Perhaps you feel flu symptoms or the like in the presence of people or places that feel uncomfortable to you. You may even decide not to buy a house or rent an apartment because you did not like the "feeling" of the place. These are all symptoms of a need for the spiritual cleansing of people, places, and things.

Removing these negative vibrations is what spiritual cleansing is all about. With this book you will be able to solve most of the problems of day to day negativity that you may encounter with people, places, and things. Through the use of spiritual cleansing you will be able to improve your own spiritual atmosphere, at home, on the job, or wherever you may find yourself. This little book is a manual of spiritual first aid, to help you clean and maintain the cleanliness of your spiritual atmosphere.

Because there is very little available material on this subject, and from a desire to provide clients and the general public with spiritual first aid information, I have undertaken to write this book. It is my intent to break new ground by providing the non-occult trained reader with simple and effective solutions to the more common spiritual problems. These solutions have been drawn from every ethnic group and spiritual practice with which I am familiar. The beer bath against Malochia comes from a witch in Hamburg, Germany, while the work with eggs comes from both Poland and Mexico. This book is not intended as a working manual for the practicing occultist; it is rather a guide for lay people who desire to improve life by keeping themselves and their environment spiritually clean.

In the 1920s, another work of this nature was published. It was written by Dion Fortune, and called *Psychic Self Defense*. It is a rather melodramatic work, written to be used by those who were students or practitioners of ceremonial magic. Although it contains some excellent suggestions, the work is aimed at those who have more than a passing familiarity with the concepts of ceremonial magic, and the control of the mind. The average person cannot work with many of the concepts presented, because he does not have the necessary training. Most of the other material available today on the subject of psychic protection seems to have been derived from her work.

If you find this information interesting enough to want to pursue the subject further, look for a teacher. The personal relationship and interaction between student and teacher is very important in learning this kind of work. Through the spiritual study that this work entails you will be able to mature, to develop self-confidence, and to test yourself. When you are ready to learn the teacher will come, and will be there as long as the student is able to learn.

Feast of St. Honoratus
1980 A.D.

Draja Mickaharic

A Word of Caution

Ⅰf an experienced spiritual practitioner finds something new in these pages, he will not deviate from the instructions given until he understands how the results are obtained. Spiritual cleansing affects the spiritual nature of the incarnate human, and until you have increased your sensitivity (through training) to the point that you understand the principle behind any particular cleansing, you should not experiment. All of the procedures in this book are simple, safe, and effective, when the directions are followed. They are all natural in their operation, and no special training or capacity is required on the part of the user. All of these cleansings have been tested in my personal practice, as well as in the work of others.

Nothing in this book will heal a physical condition, or in any way replace the skill and experience of a physician. Consult your physician for physical illnesses. This work is concerned only with spiritual conditions.

Deviating from the instructions given in this book may be harmful, and could even cause serious damage to the spiritual nature of the experimenter. For example, the baths mentioned herein are for external use only; if taken internally they could do physical damage. Because some of these things sound simple and interesting, don't get an idea to "do a variation." When you try to work "magic" using only your own enthusiasm you are treading in dangerous waters. It would be best if you followed the directions as they are presented here.

When you have finished these pages, remember that you are responsible for using this information wisely. If you decide to become a self-declared diagnostician capable of prescribing baths and ritual solutions for other people's problems, you may not be qualified to do so. When you use this information for yourself, you cannot hurt anyone. When you involve yourself in other people's lives, you may find yourself in a predicament difficult to handle. Until you have studied with a teacher and *learned the ways* of spiritual cleansing, it must be stressed that you should follow the directions exactly as they are presented in this book and avoid experimenting.

The Spiritual Man 1

That man has a body is never in question; our five physical senses give us constant testimony concerning the bodies of those around us as well as our own. We usually deal with other people in our daily lives as though we were dealing with their clothed bodies. We make an assessment of new acquaintances, customers, clients, and strangers based upon the way we view a body with our senses; the manner in which we perceive how they dress and care for their bodies is the basis for our "first impression."

The non-corporal part of man, that which is *of man,* but is not the body of man, is what is always in question. It is in dealing with this part of the species that religions are founded, spiritual practices engaged in, and scientific doubt expressed. The reason is simple: the same physical senses which give continuous testimony to the physical part of the human being give no evidence whatsoever of the non-physical part of the human being. Science, being based on the measurable, that is to say those things which are sensed by the physical senses, must deny the existence of that which cannot be measured if it is to maintain its integrity.

For our purposes we can divide the incarnate human being into these two parts, the sensory proved physical part, and the non-sensory provable spiritual part. The physical part is the province of the physical practitioner, the physician, surgeon, biologist, and so forth. His scientific training has qualified him to deal with those parts of the human being which can be measured and classified using the realm of the senses. The spiritual part is the province of the spiritual practitioner, the priest, witch, shaman, and so forth. His non-scientific training has qualified him to deal with those parts of the human being which can be explored through a measurement and classification system using the non-sensuous realms of being.

The two realms of being only come together when the practitioner of one admits puzzlement over something which seems to go out of his area of competence into the other. Yet in every human being these two realms are blended together in such a way that they work hand in hand to enable individuals to go through life in the way they do. People use both parts of their nature (physical and spiritual) in harmony in every action on this earth!

It may be said that every living thing on the earth has its own quality. This quality is the "feeling" which is often referred to as a "vibration," or an emanation, by those who are sensitive to the qualities of different things and people. The "vibration" or quality is not a physical thing, in that it cannot be measured with the human physical senses nor through the extensions of the human physical senses that are the instruments of scientific methodology. Yet the sensitive human being who has been trained to do so can use developed "spiritual senses" to identify the quality or "vibrations" of different people, places or things.

It has often been said that everything on this earth is surrounded by a spiritual energy field, but this is not to be confused with the field of magnetic flux which surrounds a magnet. The spiritual energy field, like the quality or vibration of people, places and things, is not detectable through the physical senses. Once we can make a distinction between the physical and the spiritual parts of the human constitution, it becomes easy to understand just how spiritual cleansing works.

If we can agree that every living thing carries within it its own vibration, and that the vibration results from the field of invisible energy which surrounds it, we can understand how we can use the energy of one part of the created universe to work with the human energy field and remove unwanted detritus from it. In a way, it is just like using a combination of fat and lye (that we call soap) to scrub the human physical body to remove dirt. In both cases one part of the created universe is used to remove unwanted material from the body, physical or spiritual, of an incarnate human being.

Every inanimate object—every home, building, piece of furniture, and article of clothing—carries traces of the "energy" of the animate beings to which it has been exposed. The "energies" of those who made the object, who sold it, and those who previously owned it are impregnated into the spiritual fabric (spiritual body) of everything that exists. The spiritual body of the incarnate human being interacts with the spiritual energy field of its surroundings, both in terms of people and places. A physical analogy takes place in hypnosis, for an individual can recall subtle points of his surroundings in great detail although he may not be consciously aware that he even saw the details. Our eyes interact with the physical environment in such a way that we are actually able to remember the details of the wallpaper pattern in the waiting room at the doctor's office we visited at age three. We could also recall the smells and textures of that office while hypnotized, but it is more difficult to communicate these observations to others because we lack a common standard of comparison.

No matter how much time we spend in any given physical location, our spiritual natures, as discreet observers, will recall the entire surroundings in detail. By the same token, we can look at the area and determine just what "spiritual vibrations" or traces of spiritual energy are present. We interact with our surroundings in this way, both on a physical and on a non-physical level.

Obviously, if we are to spend too much time around someone (or something) that has a strong negative vibration, we may accept it into ourselves and be affected by it. Once this occurs, our own spiritual vibration may suffer. Spiritual cleansing will remove this negative vibration and restore our own, just as washing our hands removes the dirt acquired from necessary household chores.

Years ago, this kind of information was common knowledge. It passed from one family to another, one generation to another. Today we regard some of this information as "old wives' tales" or "superstition." But it isn't. Our world has changed a great deal in the last hundred years, and even more rapidly in the last fifty. While we have gained from the scientific material progress we have made, these gains came to us at a price—the loss of some of the knowledge of our spiritual natures. We have lost a part of our "old knowledge."

We can fly from New York to Los Angeles in a matter of hours, but we also mingle our energy fields with hundreds or even thousands of people who are strangers to us. Our physical senses report the airplane flight to us in all its details, but we receive no such report of the consequences of intermingling our energy fields with so many people. Only those few people with finely attuned spiritual senses are aware of the difficulty that such mingling may bring.

In the old days we lived a quiet life. We seldom saw anyone outside the family structure. Many people lived an entire lifetime on a farm or in a small town. In 1900 many thought it was a great event to travel twice a year to a town twenty or fifty miles away in order to do the seasonal shopping. People were intimately familiar with their personal surroundings, and they kept them clean. There were few strangers among us. When strangers arrived, we knew how to cope with the energy field they brought with them. Every home had its protective charms, and every family had its household rituals.

When I was a boy growing up in a rural setting in central Europe, well over fifty years ago, it would have been unthinkable for us to go to bed until my grandmother had swept a pinch of salt out of the front door, and my grandfather had barred the doorway with the heavy bar that closed it for the night. We then said our prayers, asking God's protection on us as we slept. Only then did we retire to bed, feeling as protected and secure as if we had lived in the greatest castle in Hungary.

Protection keeps us from harm, and spiritual cleansing removes harm once it has occurred. Most families no longer have household rituals to keep them from harm, but in many ethnic groups the use of charms and talismans is still practiced. I see people from Mediterranean countries wearing the golden "horn" charm to ward off the evil eye. Many Christians wear the cross around their neck as a charm; all religions have their own form of the protective amulet.

The concept of spiritual cleansing is an integral part of religious ritual. The ritual appeals to our emotions, and we feel better after we have participated in one. We attend a Latin Mass, and come out feeling lighter and cleaner, something the vernacular mass fails to do for most of us. We may go to an Easter sunrise service, and come away feeling "like a different person." We may attend temple for Yom Kippur and feel renewed strength inside us. The cleansing we feel comes from our having accepted the religious ritual somewhere inside of us. Several days later we may begin to feel "grubby" again.

We tend to forget the significance of our religious rituals, for we participate in them in a group, and no one tells us *why* we do what we do. Years ago a person's religion signified his way of life. Today, all too often our stated religion is a "name only" philosophy. We forget about it all week and go to church or temple only for social reasons, because the ritual holds no meaning for us. Some people may know the outer meaning of the ritual of their inherited religion, but seldom know what the ritual means symbolically. Rarely do people understand the rituals connected with a religious creed other than their own. All religions have one thing in common—a ritual designed to keep the believer spiritually clean.

Most people still yearn for rituals that appeal to the forces of nature, or the forces of God, because in the old days we could worship that way. These rituals appeal to something deep inside us, and we feel better after we have participated in them. These rituals have the greatest spiritual cleansing effect on us, because they touch and stir those non-physical parts of our being of which we are not ordinarily aware.

This is a book of instruction for people who want to keep themselves clean, whether they go to church or not. Using the information supplied in this book will not interfere with any religious practice—it will enhance it. For those readers who are not involved in any group religion, these remedies will help center you in your own beliefs.

Many readers may be unfamiliar with different religious rituals. For this reason we need to consider the concept of cleansing from a religious point of view. Religious ritual is the set of practices engaged in by a specific religion. Rituals include not only the annual cycle of religious worship, but such life-event services as weddings, funerals, ordination, and others. Bar-Mitzvah, circumcision, baptism, and confirmation, which are life-event ceremonies that bring a person into the congregation of the religion are also rituals.

The general concept behind rituals is that they are actions which result in bringing someone closer to his Creator. Rituals are repetitive actions, in that the more they are repeated, the more power they acquire, and the more effective they become. For a ritual to have the effect that is desired, it must be effective on the *non-physical* level as well as on the physical level. If a person is brought closer to his Creator both physically and spiritually, he is, in the process, cleansed of any accumulated negativity he may bring to the ritual.

Roman Catholic, Orthodox Catholic, and Jewish Orthodox rituals are more complete, because these religions have a different view of the nature of God and the communion of man and God than do many of the Protestant Christian churches. Communion and Baptism are the major Protestant rituals, while the Catholic and Jewish religions have rituals for almost every possible event in the life. Yet whatever the religion or the ritual, cleansing of the spiritual nature is a part of every religious experience, even though we don't understand it any more.

One religious group native to the United States has developed a complete set of working rituals. That is the Church of Jesus Christ of the Latter Day Saints, the Mormons. They have a set of rituals specifically designed for spiritual cleansing, a "Sealing" ritual for protection against negative forces, and a training program which is second to none for spiritual practitioners in their religion. Every Mormon temple and every Mormon congregation has direct access to the services of a spiritual practitioner through an internal hierarchy. A Mormon need only ask the president of the congregation or any of the priests or elders for help and it will be made available. This is the only Christian religion in which the line of spiritual practice is so direct and open.

So-called primitive cultures have such a close tie to the concept of ritual, and the idea of the priest as spiritual practitioner, that conversion to the Christian faith is usually quite acceptable to them. This is the real reason why Christianity made such great headway among the "pagans," both in ancient and modern times. The "pagans" felt that the Christian God must be more powerful than their own, and chose to adopt it.

As people from less materialistic and less sophisticated areas of the world emigrated to the United States they brought their rituals for magic and spiritual cleansing with them. The American ethnic melting pot has resulted in an occult melting pot as well. The United States blends every ethnic practice in the world. It blends every religious practice that one could think of. The effect of these blendings often causes a dilution of cultural cleansing practices, as younger family members become involved with television, little league, and other more mundane affairs. Children of first generation emigrants usually repudiate their ancestral heritage, and the first things lost are the "hidden" family practices, including the family rituals and the process of spiritual cleansing.

While we are losing knowledge of our family and religious practices of spiritual cleansing, we are in contact with more people today than ever before. A trip to a suburban shopping center or a ride on a city subway will bring us into contact with more people who are strangers to us than our great grandparents probably ever met. In addition, the stresses of our aspiration-centered society, with its demands for material achievement, cause many people to become and remain uncentered.

We need to re-learn how to handle the manifestations of spiritual energy which come to us as we go about our daily affairs. True psychic attack is not a common occurrence, as few people are important enough to be the recipient of a psychic attack, and fewer still are well enough trained to launch one. Psychic negativity may be transmitted on a much lower level, however, and it is this negative spiritual energy which can be removed through the process of spiritual cleansing.

There are several forms of spiritual negativity that you can easily remove from yourself. One is the psychic dirt that is carried about by someone who lives life in a sea of negativity. A client of mine had a sister who had been in business out of the country for years. Her business failed and she returned to the area where her family lived. She immediately arranged a schedule of visiting in turn all of the members of her family. With her she brought her tale of woe, and made gloomy forecasts for every member of her family. My client and his wife both felt very tired after her first visit, and had an unusually troubled sleep that night. I gave him some suggestions, which he implemented, including baths and the burning of incenses mentioned later in this book. The result was that not only was her next visit less tiring, but within a few weeks the sister decided to curtail her visits to once a month rather than coming by on a weekly basis.

It is also fairly easy to rid yourself of the negative energy acquired by buying used furniture or moving into an apartment or house with "bad vibes." Another client of mine purchased an old bureau from a house which must have been full of evil vibrations. She placed the bureau in a guest room. Within a short time the room became very "dark." Suspecting something amiss, she had the bureau and the guest room cleaned spiritually. As soon as the cleansing was done, people asked if she had painted the room, it looked so bright and cheery.

You may wonder how to separate spiritual negativity coming from others and that which may be coming from yourself. This is particularly important to do if you are feeling depressed. Most mature people can look within themselves and find out why they are depressed and feeling bad. "Why am I feeling lousy?" they say—and the inner self says, "Because you just goofed up." And you know that your inner voice is right. You can back it up because you know what you've done. But what happens when you wake up feeling wonderful, and by 10 a.m. you feel lousy and can't think of one good reason why you feel that way? Your personal relationships are fine, you like your job at the moment, and you are enjoying your life. Yet you have just been overwhelmed by a feeling of depression. Perhaps you just can't stop thinking about someone, and no matter what you do, a certain person keeps coming back into your mind. Maybe it's a coworker—maybe it's a friend. This phenomena might be caused by one or both of you. A spiritual cleansing can remove a lot of depressing negative energy.

The kind of spiritual cleansing presented in this book may be considered a first-aid solution to many of the spiritual problems faced by people in their daily life. If you have a problem that you treat as indicated in this book, and you find that it doesn't change or go away, you need to seek the services of a spiritual practitioner. But at least you have the first-aid solution to the problem at your disposal.

With the foregoing in mind you might begin your study of this book. Read the entire volume before undertaking any of the cleansings. The practice of spiritual cleansing is of sufficient unfamiliarity to most people to make it worthwhile to gain as much insight as possible before beginning.

Malochia, or, "The Evil Eye" 2

A General Description

Malochia, or the Evil Eye, is a common affliction—a form of unconscious malefic practice known to all peoples, especially those from
countries bordering on the Mediterranean Sea. Although usually
involuntary in nature, it is responsible for much human suffering and
misery. Every race and culture throughout human history has its own
name for Malochia. Belief in the effects of Malochia are common and
ancient. Today people still believe in it and use the term more freely
than one might suppose.

Recorded instances of Malochia have been deciphered in the
ancient texts of Babylonia and Egypt. Certain people and animals
have been credited with the ability to cast the "glance of malice" upon
others. This "glance of malice" is in fact an energy form which has an
effect upon people and animals as well as physical objects. It is the
same variety of energy as a true curse for it has the same nature.

So widespread is the influence of Malochia that the ability to cast
it often forms part of the definition of witchcraft among those who
discuss the sociology of the practice of magic. They feel it separates

witchcraft from sorcery. Anthropologists recording the natures of so-called primitive cultures find that Malochia is both accepted as real and feared among all primitive peoples. Yet the influence of Malochia is usually denied by those who are committed to the more materialistic practices of mental and physical healing. As a result, the remedies for this common condition are not available through these channels.

The evil eye is mentioned in the Bible. Mark (7:14–23) lists the evil eye as one of the evils that comes from within that defiles man. Throughout the King James translation of the Bible, the term *evil eye* is used in the context of its root cause—envy. At the time of the translation the two phrases had almost identical meanings.

People who cast the evil eye usually find that it happens against their conscious will. They launch the attack without any conscious desire to harm. Occasionally some people learn they can cast the evil eye and are repentent—they sincerely pray to gain relief from the affliction. There are cases of such people blinding themselves to keep this spiritual affliction from being the cause of injury to their own children.

While the most common passage of the evil eye is from one marital partner to another, or from parent to child, it is not unusual to hear of people giving themselves the evil eye. This occurs when they are overly envious of either their bodies or possessions. In the myth of Narcissus, it is thought that he gave the evil eye to himself through his self-praise and adoration.

Malochia is passed when the person casting it is envious, jealous, or possessive. The act of transmitting the glance of malice is completed by looking at the person whose possessions, happiness, or good fortune is most susceptible to injury. Ancients who knew about Malochia knew they were liable to fall victim to one who casts the evil eye. It was not uncommon for those people to avoid praise, or to demean themselves while being praised. In some cultures, like Eastern ones, if you admire something in the home, it is given to you! This is done to avoid causing envy, and the eventual receipt of the evil eye.

The spiritual energy from the eyes, when malevolently charged, is what produces the effect we know as Malochia. Plutarch said that the eyes "dart out fiery rays" which strike anything looked at. His belief that the eyes send out rays which identify what is seen is based on the idea that the motion of the eye is under the conscious control of the individual's will. In this respect, eyes are a "masculine" penetrative principle, as contrasted with ears, a "feminine" receptive principle. The ears are receptive because they are available to receive any sound that strikes them. This ancient belief is the basis of all the eye discipline practices found in many different religious faiths.

In general, women, children, and the young seem to be the most frequent victims of the evil eye. In societies where the social position of women is inferior to men, it is usually felt that women cast the evil eye. In societies where women's status is not greatly inferior to that of men, it is usually attributed to both sexes. In fact, because the ability to cast Malochia is really a spiritual phenomena, there is no connection between the sex of the person and the ability to transmit it.

For the most part, Malochia escapes the physical senses while it is being transmitted. It is only when the influence begins to affect the victim that consciousness of something being wrong may take place. Few people are able to sense the transmission before it begins, and even fewer can ward it off once it has been sent. Those who are the unconscious transmitters may send the curse to a number of people over the course of a lifetime and never consciously know of the harm they do.

The intensity of this transmission of malefic energy varies greatly because of the sender. Men who could cast Malochia consciously have been known to kill trees and small animals with a glance. A number of cases have been recorded of people who cast Malochia and caused the failure of pocket calculators, stereo sets, and other electrical or mechanical devices, especially clocks and watches. Obviously, this is unconscious energy.

The Gospel of Mark relates a story about Christ cursing a fig tree for not bearing fruit out of season (Mark 11:12–14). Following his curse the fig tree withered and died, "dried up from the roots" (Mark 11:20–21). The energy used by Christ to effect this curse on a fig tree is the same as the energy of Malochia.

The symptoms from Malochia are similar to other physical illnesses. It is so common that it is the first thing a spiritual practitioner will look for. Regardless of the complaint from a client, a treatment for Malochia is usually the first treatment offered. The nature of curses and negative energies is such that the removal of Malochia is the first step in effecting any cure. The removal of this malefic energy gives the client hope.

The most frequent manifestation of Malochia is a dull headache, probably located in only one of the quarters of the victim's head. The eyes may tear, the person may feel an unusual incident of eyestrain, or his eyes may feel very tired. In more serious cases a dullness of the thought processes, a general feeling of physical disability, a lack of energy, or general tiredness accompanied by a headache may occur.

Malochia may cause a physical disability which will affect the weakest part of the body. In cases of repeated Malochia, as between husband and wife, a gradual increase in susceptibility to accidents or slight injuries may take place. Sometimes a wife who resents the sexual contact with her husband will make him impotent through repeatedly giving him Malochia. This is rare and usually happens with at least some conscious intent on the part of the wife. Practitioners with auric vision have frequently reported the tearing of the astral fabric, orbicular (a hole in the aura) wounds and similar effects from Malochia.

The most common confusion of symptoms is between repetitive Malochia and migraine headaches. A person who is the frequent recipient of Malochia from someone close will often decide he has developed chronic migraines. Only a history of the case, including any events occurring ten minutes preceding the onset of the headache, will allow an accurate diagnosis to be made by a physician or medical practitioner. A case of this sort would be better referred to a spiritual practitioner for treatment.

Every pressure headache should be treated for Malochia. The home treatment is simple, effective, and can clear the way for further work to be done. Any history of head or eye difficulties should be considered as relating to the receipt of Malochia.

Treatment

Any technique used for the cure or remission of Malochia will involve similar factors. First, one must remove the negative spiritual energy

from the afflicted person. Second, the person is blessed and the negative energy is replaced with the energy of the blessing. Objectively, this
can be compared to the removal of a splinter, for first the foreign
object is removed and then the wound can heal.

The most effective single remedy for the remission of Malochia is
a *beer bath*. It will remove all traces of simple Malochia, and at the
same time add strength to the person's spiritual body. Prepare and use
it in the following manner:

Beer Bath

1. Add about a quart of beer and a teaspoonful of table salt to
   half a tub of lukewarm water, and stir clockwise until the
   beer and water are mixed.

2. Enter the tub and immerse yourself completely several
   times. Then sit in the tub and pour the water over yourself.
   Immerse and rinse yourself with the water several more
   times until you have been in the tub six or seven minutes.
   You can use a pan or a glass to pour the water over your
   body.

3. Leave the tub and towel dry your hair, put on a bathrobe
   and allow the bath water to dry on you. You should go to the
   bedroom immediately and pray sincerely for help. The best
   prayer you can make is the Twenty-third Psalm. The Lord's
   Prayer (Matthew 6:9–13) can also be used by those who are
   believing Christians.

In fact, the prayer after the bath is as effective as the bath itself.
The removal of negative energy through the action of taking the bath
will make the prayer more effective. Most people don't know how to
pray. Only when one knows how to pray is prayer an effective antidote
to or a protection from Malochia. The instructions for true prayer are
in Matthew 6:6.

The Gospel of Matthew (see 5:43 through 7:29) gives as complete
a system of spiritual instruction as can be found anywhere. The

person who masters this instruction in theory as well as in practice in daily life will find he is placing himself beyond susceptibility to the effects of Malochia.

～の

There are other treatments for minor Malochia which can be used on a continuing basis by those who find themselves susceptible to its negative effects. These are especially useful for people who are subject to the pressure of jealousy or envy from a mate or business associate— or even a friend. The treatments may be disguised as cosmetic and the ritual can be performed on a daily basis while attempting to elevate the soul to a point where it is no longer affected.

1. We mentioned that the ears are the organs of passive receptivity while the eyes are aggressive. The symbolic cleansing of the ears can make it impossible for any evil (dirt, that part of the divine creation being where you don't want it to be) of Malochia to find a receptive place. With this in mind we can clean the ears every day with a cotton swab soaked in plain old hydrogen peroxide. This simple action will keep away the tendency to receive Malochia or at least weaken it. According to a number of people, this practice has the added virtue of making one less susceptible to the common cold.

2. Muscular tension, especially that of the upper shoulders and along the back of the neck, makes one more open to the effects of Malochia. Minor cases of "bad vibes" can open one to Malochia because the individual becomes desensitized to his environment. You can soak a teaspoon full of basil (the herb) in a bottle of ethyl rubbing alcohol and use it as a neck and shoulder rub during the day to alleviate the tension. This remedy is especially effective for women who feel the pressure of work. The back of the neck and shoulders can be wiped with the alcohol-basil mixture on a bit of cotton or tissue.

3. A cool shower is an excellent way to rid oneself of negativity, tension, or concerns that are absorbed during the day. If you take a cool shower as soon as you return from work, you'll notice you won't have as much tension in your domestic life. The concerns of the workday world will go down the drain and you'll be in fine humor during the evening.

4. A morning tub bath, with a teaspoon of sea salt in the water, is useful for the removal of light negative vibrations of all kinds as well as weak forms of Malochia. Sea salt can be obtained in health food stores and in some grocery stores.

5. A quarter teaspoon of cinnamon added to about three or four tablespoons of talcum powder makes a mixture that prevents envy and jealousy from others. The powders should be well mixed and applied to the sternum, between the breasts, every morning after bathing. Only a small amount of this powder is used. You want protection; you do not want to end up smelling like a cinnamon gumdrop.

Charms and Other Protections Against Malochia

There are a number of charms and other physical protections that have been used in different cultures to protect against the effects of Malochia. One of the most common is the horn, made of gold or plastic, which is often worn by members of the ethnic Italian community for this purpose. "Horse Brasses," variously configured shapes of cast brass formerly worn on the harnesses of horses, were first used to protect the animals wearing them from Malochia.

Other cultures also use a variety of objects for this purpose. These charms include the carved "Fig," a small carved hand, held in a certain way, and the "Stones," a charm of alternating pieces of coral and jet. Most of these charms are worn around the neck on a necklace. Any amulet or talisman worn by a person, which attracts the attention of other people, may be more or less effective against Malochia. The real effectiveness of such charms and amulets is always dependent, at least to some extent, on the beliefs of the person using it.

I once had a salesman tell me that round objects distracted the sight of a person who was being spoken to, while rectangular objects did not. Because of this, he never wore any round or oval object when making sales calls. On the other hand, this distraction of attention is the primary effect of any charm worn to protect against Malochia. The person who is speaking to the wearer of the charm usually has his attention distracted by the charm. The intention of the charm is that any feelings of envy or jealousy will be directed to the charm being worn, rather than to the person wearing it.

There are a few other things which can also be done to prevent the effects of Malochia from penetrating the individual who is the recipient of the glance. The most effective single action is that of prayer. Pray for protection throughout the day—the best time to do this is when you get up in the morning. Sincere prayers are always answered.

You can wear a cord around your waist as an effective means of sealing off your aura. Women can do this by wearing a knotted belt (either over or under clothing) and tying it in a square knot in front of the body. Men can use a good grade of cotton twine tied around the waist in the same way—but under the clothing.

Wearing a blessed crucifix or other religious charm is effective if you are a sincere devotee of the religious practice represented. If you don't believe in the efficacy of the charm there is no point in wearing one as it won't work.

Occasionally charms, amulets, and religious symbols worn specifically for protection from Malochia will break or disappear. It is best to let them go as the destruction is proof that they served the purpose. They should be replaced when they break, but the injured charm or amulet should be allowed to *remain where it has fallen.* That means don't pick it up!

In addition to the beer bath previously mentioned, there are many other ways to remove Malochia. Most (like the German beer bath) are specifically cultural—from a particular ethnic tradition. Some are restricted in their application, or may be taught only under specific circumstances. One method for cleansing comes from southern Italy and may be taught only to a person of the opposite sex as the clock strikes midnight bringing in the New Year!

Whether one prefers baths to prayer is a matter of choice or belief. The beer bath is probably the most effective method for removing Malochia by yourself. As in all cases, if the first aid remedy doesn't provide a permanent relief, further treatment may be required. If the beer bath provides only slight relief, it should be repeated frequently until a spiritual practitioner can be consulted. First aid is first aid—it has its place—but it cannot heal desperate or chronic cases.

Protection While Asleep 3

A side from Malochia, the most prevalent spiritual difficulty which affects humankind might be called *Influence while asleep*. This phrase covers a wide variety of spiritual complaints and we shall discuss the most common of them. Before considering the remedies for sleep problems, we need to discuss the causes. It is important that you understand the function of sleep as well.

Sleep

Sleep provides the period of rest for both the conscious mind and the animal body. During sleep, the spiritual nature is allowed some freedom, much like a prisoner being released on parole. The analogy is correct! During "life" the spirit, that part of the human construction generally known as the *soul*, is actually a prisoner of the flesh. When the soul incarnates, *it* takes a body, so we are actually souls that possess a body, not bodies that possess a soul.

The soul is the real, immortal and eternal part of the human construction. The body is only the transitory and expendable part of us.

So sleep becomes a period of freedom for the soul, a daily vacation from the drudgery of existence in the flesh. Modern scientific medical research has shown the importance of adequate sleep for human beings. People who are deprived of sleep suffer more frequently from psychological difficulties than those who have adequate and restful sleep. Sleep deprivation has been found to be a real and often seriously debilitating medical phenomenon.

Once we look at sleep from this spiritual perspective, it becomes obvious that the suspension of consciousness mutes the thinking, logical, rational, or critical faculties (which we call the mind) so we can accept the spiritual nature. Or return to it for a while at least. The conscious mind tends to resist the temptations offered from the spiritual realms because to accept them would indicate that "consciousness" is not completely conscious. A serious mental imbalance could arise in the person who makes this unexpected realization.

Because our spiritual nature is most open to influence during sleep, the general phrase *influence while asleep* describes all cases. But in fact, the influence may have been presented to the individual during the waking state, and only manifests when he goes to sleep. In this way, it might be compared to a cat who watches a mouse, and who jumps only when the mouse relaxes his guard.

When we can't sleep, something is wrong. Our soul nature is not able to have its free time. Normally, when we can't sleep, friends say we must be anxious about something. That may be true, and when the possibility of anxiety is explored consciously, we may discover what keeps us from sleeping. Solving the problem often brings us restful sleep. Sometimes we can't sleep even after we may think we have consiously solved the problems. This is when we a should begin to consider the possibilities of some kind of psychic or non-physical influence affecting us while we sleep. Sometimes we may get strong hints as to what is actually happening to us from our dreams.

The Dream State

Everybody has an explanation for their dreams. Dreams are a popular and curious subject. We can't explain them easily. Let's discuss the possibility of other things taking place when the dream or so-called dream occurs.

Lower Astral Plane

The freedom the soul feels when released during sleep should not be confused with lower astral experiences. When the spirit prefers to dwell in this area, the dwelling place can be a source of delight to the unevolved, and it might be difficult to turn aside from temptations which are offered at that level. The lower astral temptations translated into the daylight reality of waking consciousness are sometimes perceived as dreams. Occasionally they represent what we call *influence while asleep.*

For example, lower astral dreams may often be nothing more than wishful thoughts on the part of the dreamer. Sometimes they are merely the mutual entertainment of two dreamers who delve into things in spirit that they would find inappropriate in the flesh. They may also be the result of released tensions from the individual's subconscious. This subconscious release of emotional tension in our dreams is the very foundation of the art of psychoanalysis. The more the dreams symbolize a release of tension, or the subconscious release of any kind of energy, the more vivid the dream becomes to the dreamer.

In the case of a dream involving forbidden experience, the dream state consumes energy from the person's vital force. This energy need not be expended in the dream state, but rather should be used by the person during a normal, waking day. The expenditure of our vital force in negative directions is what we seek to limit when we wish to control the influence which comes to us when we are asleep.

At this point it should be said that vivid dreams—those we find easy to remember when we awaken—represent a release of energy from the astral (non-physical) body. This is usually the result of a memory which represents a releasing of negative emotional energy, often from an emotional block within ourselves. Jungian analysts, and others, encourage patients who dream to release energy in this way. They may not discuss the "astral body" but the result is the same. The purpose of the dreaming experience is to clean the unconscious memory of blocked energy, resolving and releasing it. Mental and spiritual clarity results from either successful psychological or spiritual treatment—and will be the end result of any properly conducted spiritual training.

Magic and Demons

We hear many stories about astral demons, psychic attacks, monsters from the deep, and all sorts of negative influences that appear when we sleep. The vast majority of these stories are based on personal guilts, fears, self-deceptions, greed, and even pathological disturbances within the individual who considers himself the victim of these disturbing and often traumatic dreams. The conscious conception of right and wrong in each of us is taught to the subconscious mind as we grow from child to adult. The subconscious concept of right and wrong calls certain negative forces to us. Delusion and self-deception in this area can be more of a comfort to oneself than dealing with divine reality when one is unaware of what divine reality is. Those who suffer from the "monsters" will seek help when the time comes. Help can come via psychoanalysis, a spiritual practitioner, the "right" class, or the "right" teacher.

One also hears of the attack by the "famed black magician." Should you, for some unlikely reason, be singled out for attack by a trained and powerful magician, you will probably never know it. In the rare event that this should occur, you would probably march steadfastly toward the goals set for you, with little hope or chance of changing your course. When you are marching to his drum you may be entirely convinced that you are doing everything *you* desire and that your actions always represent your own best interests. The only clue that something might be wrong with a person under this kind of attack, is that the individual experiences absolutely no difficulties or troubles in life. All goes perfectly well as he answers to the sound of his new master's voice. As this is not often considered to be a negative state in human affairs, it is very difficult to persuade anyone that he has any problems at all.

There are a number of cases that could be cited to show this sort of influence, but they are really unbelievable! Unless one has studied this field or actually experienced the situation, stories about magical ability are not something one can accept as real. To strangers, the person under the spell looks really successful and perfectly normal.

Psychic Attack

Generally, psychic attack is not nearly so intriguing as the above mentioned dreams of demons, monsters, and evil black magicians. Several kinds of psychic attack can take place while the victim is asleep, and we shall discuss the most common and frequent of them. These nocturnal attacks are not usually deliberate, they are not uncommon, and they are usually not hard to resolve.

The Average Magician

When a self-proclaimed magician decides to attack or attempt to control another human being, a lower order of magical skill is being manifested. And the effect is entirely different than that of the proficient magician because you know you are under attack. You know something is wrong and ultimately you will attempt to fight the energy. In these cases, the victim may have nightmares, dreams, restless sleep, or see vivid frightening apparitions or other kinds of phenomena. Hints and comments from associates may prompt a strong self-examination. The feeling that one is under an attempted influence from others may cause the individual to seek a spiritual practitioner. The person being attacked may even change his sleep patterns.

The Psychic Take-over

Another manifestation of *influence while asleep* occurs when one wakes with thoughts that are foreign to the waking consciousness. This is a different experience than waking with fragments of a dream on your mind. The remnants of a dream may also be present, but in addition to the dream, you may be thinking about a certain individual. The memory may give a clue to who is trying to influence your sleep. People who may try to influence you may not even be conscious of doing it. These people may be insecure, you may be important to them, you may frighten them, you may represent something to them that you don't even know about. The important thing about psychic protection is that you don't have to be concerned with the motive of the person affecting you. The important thing is to clean your living space, so that you can do what you want without being unduly influenced by someone else.

The "take-over" influence has many causes and is no less varied in its effects. While the most predominant effect is a sapping of vitality, the symptoms can vary from a feeling of increasing lassitude to a victim's gradual dedication of his life to another person. The victim may even become involved in a cause—even a humanitarian cause. The clue is that the person makes changes in action or behavior that are unexplanable.

For example, one of my clients became extremely clumsy and began to have all kinds of minor accidents—with the car, accidents on the job, falling upstairs, and so on. In this case, investigations revealed that a coworker was attempting to take over his job. The coworker was using magic on him which manifested during sleep.

Another client, a young lady, was relatively successful in life. She suddenly became interested in a man she had known for a long time, one who had never interested her before. The man did not seem to respond to her attentions. She couldn't understand herself, and in the process of treatment it was discovered that her girlfriend wanted to be with the man my client had dated for years. The girlfriend tried (through magic) to push her friend into the arms of a new man, leaving the one she wanted available to her. The case was even more interesting when the unresponsive male came in as a client to try to understand what was happening to him! He noticed my female client's interest in him, did not understand why he was not attracted to her, and couldn't understand why she was willing to leave her boyfriend to take up with him. Many times these kinds of activities are not done consciously. Most people don't realize the strength of their thought projections, whether conscious or unconscious.

In order to avoid the psychic take-over, we need to understand something about the mind. Thoughts that enter the mind are rarely of our own conscious selection. We respond to the thoughts of other people all the time. Because this happens so often, it makes it difficult for us to diagnose ourselves. To learn if we are influenced by outside forces, we need to be alert to clues that come from others. Our friends and acquaintances may comment about tiredness, a change in our attitude, a change in personality, or other changes that we have made in our lives. These comments, if we are alert enough to hear them, can inform us of the possibility of these external influences.

The Psychic Vampire

The psychic vampire is not someone who drinks your blood! The psychic vampire is rather a person who sucks away your energy. These kinds of experiences are not uncommon at all—everyone knows someone who "drains" him—the person who calls on the phone and talks and talks—and when you get off the phone you want to take a nap. Or you go and visit "Aunt Mary" and when you leave you think you are getting flu symptoms. Many people who drain others of energy are completely unconscious that they are doing it.

In regard to *influence while asleep,* the vampire is a weak individual who draws the vital energy from someone who is stronger. The end result of this kind of vampirism manifests in a victim who awakens feeling tired and restless after what should have been a good night's sleep. For the first few hours after waking, the person often feels crabby, irritable, or may experience a general lack of focus.

We can begin to look for clues when we feel the symptoms. And when we have conversations during the waking hours with the psychic vampire type, we begin to learn who this person is. And then we are ready to protect our bedrooms at night, so our vital energy is not drained away from us.

Visits from the No-longer Living

Occasionally an individual has a vivid dream or series of dreams about a deceased friend or family member. This is sometimes a sign that the spirit of the departed is attempting to communicate with the living. If the dreams have no point, if they contain no message, it may be that the deceased friend or relative is simply presenting himself for no reason. The individual may also be obsessed about the departed person for reasons of his or her own. Having a few of these dreams is a good reason for the dreamer to look into him- or herself and see just what his or her relationship to the departed was and how it can be moderated. Praying for the peace of the departed is always a good idea, but it is especially worthwhile to pray for those of the departed whom you have dreams about.

If the individual is not "drawing" the spirit of the departed to them, the problem can be solved without difficulty. The *mothball treatment* will cause any persistent spirit to lose energy. This treatment will not hurt him, for he will not lose his vital force, but he will leave you alone. See the section on mothball treatments later in this chapter.

Sexual Dreams

When you have vivid romantic feelings, or wake up remembering dreams that include romantic episodes with another person, it is possible that you actually experienced these romantic episodes in the realm of spirit. The sexual interlude is usually only presented to the conscious mind if it is willing to receive such information. These experiences are the source of the wonderful tales about sexual spirits, Incubus and Succubus, who engage in spectacular sexual bouts with the not-so-unwilling.

For the most part, such episodes, even when the dream includes an orgasm, do not involve a person you know. The partner is usually a total stranger. When you know the partner in your sexual dream, that in itself is no guarantee that you experienced the episode with his or her astral equivalent. More important, it is also not a guarantee that the person you dream of has any knowledge of the dream you shared in such a personal sense. Anyone who has had strong sexual dreams should be aware of these facts. Knowing these things can save a great deal of embarrassment in your conscious waking life!

The delights experienced during these astral liaisons are not particularly beneficial to the person who wishes to become more spiritual. The experience can be avoided by a sincere prayer as one falls asleep.

A bit of salt and holy water can be added to the bed between the sheets. (See section under Consecrated Salt.) If these remedies fail, it becomes necessary to look within to learn why the experiences keep happening. Maybe you are drawing them to you for a reason.

Treatment of Conditions

Treatment of spiritual conditions caused by *influence while asleep* is a multifaceted affair. Several preventive measures should be adopted as a part of the regular nightly ritual. Other measures can be taken from time to time when one feels the need for them. We get signals from the outside world and we can heed these signals. For example, a signal might be indicated by having a quarrel with an associate at work, a run-in with a relative with a bad temper, an urge to keep your eyes open even though you are exhausted.

The main thing to remember is that the fundamental precautions are simple—so simple that anyone can do them as a part of the nightly bedtime ritual. These basic protections should become as familiar as brushing your teeth. And when you feel the need for a heavier protection, other rituals can be added for the time you feel they are necessary. You don't need them anymore when you feel you don't need them. A balance should be arrived at   protection should not become paranoia.

Water—The Basic Remedy

The first effort in prevention of *influence while asleep* is to provide a vessel for the reception of energy from the influence. This can be accomplished by adopting a nightly ritual known as *sleeping with water*. This ritual is so basic that many have done it from childhood without having any conscious knowledge of why it is done.

Immediately before retiring for the night, fill a glass with water and place it at the head of your bed, so that it will be beside you when you sleep. This glass of water is not drinking water—it is there to catch all the energy you don't want around you. This glass should never be used for drinking water. In the morning, empty the water in the toilet and rinse out the glass three times, pouring the water used to rinse it into the toilet as well. When you flush it down, you are flushing away what was in the glass.

Repeat this ritual every night, and you will find that much of the difficulty attaining good sleep disappears. If you feel that your sleep is still troubled at times, you might add a few bits of camphor to the water every night. A piece as large as a wooden match-head will do as well as any larger amount. More doesn't necessarily work better. The energy released by the dispersion of the camphor will assist in the dissipation of any thought forms.

It really makes no difference which hand you use to draw the water to fill your glass every night, but in the morning you should take the glass in your anti-dexter hand. (This is opposite to the hand you write with. If you are right-handed, your anti-dexter hand is your left.) By using this hand and following this procedure, you are stressing the symbolism of refusing to take back that which the water has collected during the night.

Consecrated Salt

This may be obtained at any Roman Catholic Church, and a pinch of consecrated salt between the sheets on your bed will be of assistance in "earthing" you, and keeping your nightly expeditions to the astral realms under some control. Sprinkling your bedsheets with holy water will also help—but it is recommended only if you sleep alone. Holy water can be obtained from a church or religious supply store.

Since the reformation of the Roman Catholic Ritual following the Second Vatican Conference and the abandonment of the Latin Mass, there has been a decline in the belief in the efficacy of the consecration of salt, oil, and water in the Roman Catholic priesthood. The act of consecration, theological opinion to the contrary, is individually dependent upon the ability of the incarnate human soul who performs it. If you want holy water or consecrated salt, it can be purchased in a church supply store, or you can ask a priest to make it for you. You may want to ask a certain priest to perform the consecration because you feel he has the ability to do it. Experience will show you that some priests do a better job of consecration than others.

Consecrated salt or holy water added to the bed between the sheets is particularly helpful in ridding oneself of sexual dreams. If this practice doesn't help, if the dreams occur too often and are not cured by looking within, the dreams can be avoided by using prayer. A sincere prayer offered just before sleep will lift the soul to a different plane.

Sea Salt

This is a very useful remedy when dealing with invalids or children. It cleans the air. Sea water is wonderful to keep the psychic dreck away. When we are not close to the ocean, salt water becomes a problem. Sea salt can be obtained from health food stores. A pinch of it usually is enough, in the bath or between the bedsheets.

Mothballs

Mothballs can be purchased in any grocery store. They help keep a room free of unwanted psychic intrusions. Three mothballs should be placed in each corner of the bedroom. These mothballs dissipate the energy of any spirit who might attempt to influence you while you sleep. Spirits can see the effect of these mothballs. They will usually not even enter a room in which they have been placed.

If you have a serious problem with spirits in your home, you might try placing three mothballs in all of the corners of your home or apartment. This includes placing them in the closets as well. I have found that this practice is almost as effective as a full-scale cleansing and sealing of a home or apartment. It certainly is discouraging to spirits, thought forms, and astral phenomena of all kinds.

Volatile Substances

Any volatile substance placed in the corner of a room will assist in clearing the room of spirit influences. It must be noted that volatile substances usually burn, so a selection must be made which will not add a fire hazard to the home. Mothballs and camphor are fairly safe.

Flammable liquids are a fire hazard, and must be used with great care if at all.

Turpentine poured in shot glasses may be placed in the corners of a room slept in by an individual who is overly susceptible to nightmares, the effects of nature spirits, or the forces of nature.

Acetone, splashed on a wall next to a bed will effectively seal the wall from astral visitors for a week or so. It will also do grave damage to any wall covering, paint, or wallpaper! Whiskey, rum, or ethyl rubbing alcohol can be mixed fifty-fifty with water and will do almost as well with considerable less damage.

Acetone that has been colored with black India ink can be placed in small closed bottles in the corners of a room to discourage spirit visitors. This remedy discourages the spirit visitor by confusing his sense of direction. The charm works better when properly prepared with other ingredients and "worked" by a spiritual practitioner, but using acetone and ink alone is not without effect.

Mate is an herb used as a beverage in South America. Mate tea is also very discouraging to spirits, particularly spirits of the dead. If you have walls that may be washed, adding a cup of ammonia to the wash water will result in a wall that has few non-physical influences left on it. If you then rinse the clean wall with a solution of Mate tea in water, (about a cup of the tea to a gallon of water) you will find that it will discourage spirits of the dead for six to nine months. This solution will keep them out of the room in which you sleep, or away from your house, if that is your desire.

Helping the Invalid

When we try to help others, we must first be sure that we are not trying to control them. However, those who are ill need to husband all their strength and they tend to get as much energy as possible from other members of the household. The time spent in sleep should be used to accumulate and restore strength. The ill draw energy from others, especially children. This energy loss can be avoided by placing a bowl of water under the sick person's bed. If you desire, a pinch of sea salt can be added to the water in the bowl. The bowl should be emptied and rinsed daily while the invalid is awake, in the same manner as you would empty water used for protection while sleeping. Occasionally this practice will have a beneficial effect on the invalid. For the most part it will assist in maintaining the energy level. It must be noted that this practice, while spiritually beneficial, has no curative power for any illness, and a physician should be called to treat the illness of the body.

Placing three mothballs in each corner of the room in which someone is bedridden is also a good practice to follow, especially if the person is elderly. It will calm the mind and promote rest. In many cases, it will allow the person to have a deeper and more restful sleep. At the same time, the mothballs discourage the drawing of energy from other household members by the invalid. Combining the use of mothballs with the bowl of water under the bed may assist the invalid in regaining his health, but this is neither a cure-all nor a treatment for a physical condition.

Helping Children

All children go through changes for they live in the two worlds—one world being comfortable with the natural part of themselves, the other trying to be a part of the adult world.

Some children go through a period when they have terrible nightmares, see monsters, or become afraid to go to sleep. When this happens, sleeping with water, or using a bowl of water under the bed and a pinch of sea salt in the bed can be of great assistance. If this doesn't help, turpentine can be used in the corners of the room. It should be poured into four shot glasses (filled half full) and carefully placed in the room. It should not be left there after seven days. Dispose of the turpentine in the toilet or in a safe place.

Some children become overly attached to the forces of nature. Some become so involved with these elemental forces that they talk only to rocks, or rain, fire, and earth spirits, leaving other children and even parents alone. One remedy is to cover the area around the child's bed with lettuce leaves. Do this every night for seven consecutive nights. The lettuce must be swept up and discarded in the morning as soon as the child is awake. When this ritual is completed, mothballs should be placed in the corners of the room. A bowl of sea water is also put under the bed every night for a month or so. It must be emptied and rinsed every morning, and replaced with fresh water every night. This ritual can occasionally produce some dramatic cures in children who would rather play with sticks and stones than with other children. Those who do not respond to this treatment will require professional help from a psychologist or a psychiatrist. In some cases a spiritual practitioner may be of assistance in solving the child's problem.

Help for Yourself

For a peaceful rest it is occasionally advisable to fumigate your bedroom with incense before going to sleep. This is a good idea when you are having difficulty with neighbors, relatives, or friends who might feel a bit vengeful toward you. It is also a good idea to fumigate your bedroom if you have just ended a relationship with a lover. The best incense for this purpose is a blend of frankincense and benzoin. This blend has the quality of bringing more spiritual and beneficial influences close to you as you sleep. These influences will keep more negative ones away. Complete instructions for using this incense are given in chapter 7.

The Power of Prayer

When one desires restful sleep without interference from the spiritual forces in the universe, it must be remembered that prayer is the best all around solution to the basic difficulties that life on earth offers. If an individual offers sincere prayer for the elevation of his soul as he sleeps, asking that his spirit ascend the higher spheres so that it may learn and grow, he will find that he gradually gains the elevation of the spirit and the protection that he seeks. Sincere prayers are always answered, and if one prays for something, and develops a sincere desire for it, knowing that he has received it in his heart, the opportunity for the true reception of his desires will be his.

It is because our prayers are answered that occultists say that we should be certain that we know what we want before we pray. We may get it!

Cleansing with Baths 4

Some History and Background

As we have seen in the two previous chapters, the act of bathing can be used to promote spiritual as well as physical cleanliness. That this is a valid concept can be observed in major religious practices. It is implicit in the Christian ritual of baptism, where the stain of the sin of Adam is removed. The Moslem act of washing before prayers demonstrates the intention of coming to God in a state of cleanliness. Spiritual bathing implies that water washes away those things that are not wanted, whether our dirt is physical or a spiritual influence.

While most Christians can accept the concept of baptism as a spiritual cleansing, it seems more difficult to accept the idea that baths can be beneficial when taken with the intent to clean oneself spiritually. The Christian Church has experienced changes in theology within the last fifty years and many of the clergy no longer view the act of baptism as one with magical or "extra-physical" meaning. If we accept the concept of a magical cleansing ritual, then Christ's baptism by John must have been the beginning of the initiation that prepared him to be the Messiah.

The story of Christ's initiation is told in the Gospel of Matthew (3:13–4:11). Jesus presents himself to John for baptism. He is full of humility, despite the fact that John recognizes Jesus as his moral superior. This initiation is very similar to that of Apollonius of Tyana and the Mysteries of Elysium. A comparison to the initiation stories will reveal the nature of *initiation*.

Initiation has a real purpose, and due to the nature of incarnation on earth, initiation must be performed on earth in each and every lifetime, regardless of the individual's past life initiations or even present life "astral initiations of the spirit." Initiation always involves a practice, a particular way of belief, or a specific way of doing spiritual work. As this relates to a particular incarnation on earth, in order to be valid an initiation must be done in the flesh.

Initiations should never be entered into hastily. The best initiations are done only when the potential initiate is quite familiar with the path, and the practice, into which he is being initiated. In some cases, this may mean that the student has been associated with that practice, and the person who will initiate him, for three or four years. If someone tells you that you should run toward an initiation, you will probably be far better off if you run in the other direction.

When we use something natural to assist ourselves in the act of spiritualization, we are working in harmony with the will of God. Everything on this earth is given to be used for the processes required for our spiritual growth—in the personal sense as well as for the entire species. Man, being a microcosm of the divine macrocosm, must take those things which he requires from outside of himself, and add that influence to himself to gain the destiny he seeks. This is the destiny God created for him, although he may not be immediately conscious of it.

Ritual bathing only means that we are willing to share in an experience not immediately of the flesh. We take a cleansing bath, praying to clean ourselves of any spiritual (or unseen) influence that may be an unwelcome part of our aura. The ritual, in itself, indicates that we (no matter what our age) are still open enough to ask the universe (or God) to help us change what we think needs to be changed. It implies a willingness to listen to that voice within, or the voice of spiritual development—and we become trusting in something outside of our intellectual minds. Christ said we would not enter the kingdom except we be as little children (Matthew 18:1–6). And that can be interpreted as being innocent enough to *trust*. The act of ritual bathing implies the beginning of that trust.

What the Ritual Bath Can Do

A bath taken to cleanse or protect a person spiritually, or for any other spiritual or religious purpose, is different from a bath taken to remove the dirt of daily life. Because of the difference, basic rules should be followed when taking a bath intended to produce spiritual or religious effects.

When taking a spiritual bath, do not use soap, bath oil, or any other ingredients. Once the bath is prepared, you are entering into a spiritual experience, and the ritual requires that you mentally separate regular bathing and the bathing of the mind or spirit.

You can buy prepared baths or you can make your own. In the following pages, we will discuss how to make baths at home using herbs and nuts as well as other common household items. The baths listed here are helpful in dealing with basic spiritual problems any individual may encounter. These descriptions by no means cover the field. The important thing to remember is that you don't want to "make up" a bath unless you know what you are doing. Each recipe evokes certain energies. It is your obligation to use this information in a responsible way. Unless you have studied enough to go any further, it is recommended that you follow instructions precisely.

Some people prefer working with already prepared baths. If you look in the Yellow Pages of your local telephone directory, you may find a shop that sells incense, oils, and candles in the Religious Supplies section. Occasionally the prepared baths found in such a store are very effective. White baths usually have the most spiritual vibrations. In order to select the proper bath for yourself, you could ask the owner of the store to recommend one or you can look for one that appeals to you. These baths are primarily used by Spanish-speaking peoples, but as they have become more popular in the English-speaking community, the labels now appear in both Spanish and English. Even if you don't purchase a bath, you may enjoy visiting this kind of a store. The most popular bath sold is the love bath. However, we have instructions for making our own.

A Note of Caution

Spiritual baths cleanse the spirit and the soul. They help heal the wounds the soul is suffering and can help promote the healing of your being. *Spiritual baths cannot heal any physical ailment.* Do not use these baths to heal any so-called physical condition you may have. If you have any physical illness, consult your physician for treatment.

Open wounds of any kind, including surgical incisions, preclude taking tub baths. Do not immerse yourself in water for at least two weeks following any kind of surgery. If you have had surgery, follow the directions given by your doctor as to when tub baths can be taken again. No matter what he says to the contrary, spiritual baths of any kind should be avoided for at least two weeks. After that period, with the permission of your doctor, tub baths can be taken for six weeks following surgery if the incision is not wet. In this case, you will not be able to fully immerse yourself as you must keep the incision dry and covered. Most people use a plastic bag of some sort, either as a bandage or as a container to protect the area of the incision. Follow the doctor's directions exactly.

Baths cannot heal any condition that needs physical surgery. If a medical remission occurs through the action of the spiritual bath, it is a miraculous remission and cannot be attributed to the action of the bath itself. Spiritual causes of physical problems that are attempting to manifest can yield to spiritual treatment. Problems that have already manifested physically *may* yield to treatment of a spiritual nature, but remission of the problem in the average person is more of a miracle than any action a healer is able to bring about because of an act of will. There are laws of the spirit as well as laws of the physical universe, and seeking physical cures from healers is usually a waste of time and money. Any healer or spiritual practitioner who tells you that you can be cured of any manifested physical condition is telling an untruth. Give to the doctor that which belongs to him.

Preventive treatment is another story, for we can work on curing a spiritual "possible cause" only before manifestation. There are a number of baths designed to promote physical healing, but they operate by removing the spiritual cause for the illness. They remove those influences surrounding the physical body which are adverse to physical health. They have no affect whatsoever on any manifested physical condition.

Water

Water has always been the symbol of life. As the moving essence of life, water has the capacity to cleanse us of those spiritual blocks and accumulations that we acquire during a lifetime. The division of the waters mentioned in Genesis 1:6 reveals a concept that was already ancient at the time scholars tell us the scriptures were written. In ancient Babylonia, the two kinds of water were known as EA-AE. In modern English, we call them fresh (or sweet) water and salt water. The two waters have different effects on us.

Sea water, for Christian, Jew, and Moslem alike, has been charged to remove or receive all the evils of the earth, taking away what is negative and holding it. On the other hand, fresh water gives us what we need to sustain life on earth. Baths taken to remove negative influences should have water and salt, if not sea water, in their composition. Baths intended to assist or to sustain us on earth should be made with fresh water.

Christian holy water is made of blessed or consecrated salt and water. This combination is used to keep adverse influences away from us. One of the most efficacious baths the sincere Christian can take is one containing some holy water.

How to Take a Ritual Bath

First of all, be aware that a ritual bath is not intended to clean you of the physical dirt accumulated by being alive. If you want to take a ritual bath, first take a shower or bath to remove the grime. Then clean out the tub or shower, so that you come to the ritual bath with a clean tub. The desire for a spiritual bath relates to the spiritual nature and the tub should be clean of any traces of the physical world. The clean atmosphere could be extended to include a clean bathroom as well.

Prepare the bath itself. If you choose an herb or nut bath, or one of the *household formulas* discussed in this chapter, the formula has to be prepared. If you use a bath purchased in a religious supply store, all you need to do is clean yourself and the bathroom, and you are ready to proceed.

Fill the bath tub about half full of lukewarm or cool water. Pour the bath preparation into the water while the bath is being drawn. If you are using a prepared bath, rinse the bottle at least twice. If you are using a homemade herbal tea bath, strain the preparation into the tub using a tea strainer. (This will ease the strain of herbs clogging the drainpipes.)

Enter the bathtub nude, and immediately immerse yourself, head included, in the water. If these instructions seem facetious, let me assure you they are not! One of the guiding lights of modern psychology admitted he had never taken either a bath or shower nude in his entire life, and had no intention of doing so. Many women do not bathe nude, and some who do have never immersed the head in any bath water. Nude bathing, and immersion of the head, including the hair, are fundamental requirements of a spiritual bath.

If you wish, you may rinse out your mouth with the bath water. Avoid swallowing any of the bath solution, however. Be certain that the bath water enters every part of the body. If you wish, you can wet a clean washcloth with the bath solution and scrub yourself with it during the bath. Remember, you don't use soap.

You should remain in a spiritual bath for at least six to eight minutes for it to have the best effect. In certain baths, the individual may need to soak for a longer period of time. Some baths may make the person taking it feel as if six or eight minutes is a long time. A clock may be placed near the tub to insure that you bathe the proper time. Use a mechanical clock or timer rather than an electric clock.

Pray for the effectiveness of the bath as you pour the water over yourself or wash with the washcloth. Continue to immerse and wash yourself until the bath has elapsed. (You can use a clean glass to pour water over you.) Prayer is important here, for the concentration of your thoughts to the matter you wish to develop is aided by prayer. Don't let your mind wander.

When you leave the tub, wrap your hair in a towel but don't dry it. Put on a bathrobe—to cover your wet body, but don't towel dry. It is important that your body dry in the air. If you live in a warm enough place, you can stay nude until the air completely dries you—for you want the aftereffect of the bath to stay on your body. Don't bathe or wash your hair for 24 hours following a bath for spiritual improvement.

Whether or not you notice any change after a spiritual bath, rest assured the bath has had its effect. The effect is on spiritual levels of consciousness, not on the physical one. Unless you have conscious access to the level of spiritual sensation you may only notice that you feel "lighter" after the bath. Skepticism or disbelief in the effect of the bath will decrease the chance that it will be of benefit.

The Holy Water Bath

As we said before, Christian holy water is made of blessed or consecrated salt and water. The bath can be used by one who is a sincere Christian, and aids in spiritual development. Holy water can be purchased in a religious supply store and sometimes from a Catholic Church store. It can also be blessed by your priest. It cannot be made at home.

Use 6 to 8 ounces of holy water to a tub of bath water. Pray for spiritual cleansing while you are bathing. Immerse yourself in the tub several times. Stay in the tub 6 to 8 minutes. The Lord's Prayer should be recited in the tub at the end of the bath.

When using this bath, it is helpful if you have some time alone afterward. Try to arrange the bath time so you can go to your room and be undisturbed for fifteen minutes or so. If that is impossible, staying in the bathroom for the meditation time is helpful as well. If you don't have the time or the privacy, the bath will still work.

8888888888

However, prayerful meditation will make the bath have a more lasting effect on you.

The Spiritual Cleansing Bath

Baths for the removal of negative influences are legion, and they vary based on the kind of negative influences present. One general cleansing bath does no harm if the directions are followed exactly. This bath will often clear up minor spiritual difficulties.

Bath Number One

Use a clean glass one-quart jar. In it mix:

   1 cup of tap water or sea water
   1 tablespoon of household ammonia
   1 teaspoon salt
   Add another cup of water (the same as above)

   Add the contents of the jar to a half tub of water and bathe for five minutes with three immersions. Pray for release of the negative influence. Unless your skin is extraordinarily sensitive, you will have no adverse effects from the ammonia. Should you feel your skin is very sensitive and might be affected, do not take this bath!

Bath Number Two

This bath will also remove negative influences of various kinds. It is a tonic for the hair and skin as well. It has been used as a cosmetic bath so those with sensitive skin need not be apprehensive unless they know they are sensitive to vinegar. Mix:

   1 cup apple cider vinegar
   1 teaspoon salt

   Add this combination to half a tub of water and bathe for at least 5 minutes with a minimum of three full immersions. Pray for the release of any negative energy around you or for freedom from any negative influence or worry you may feel.

Bath Number Three

This bath relates even more directly to physical cleansing. While it has definite spiritual cleansing properties, it is also a bath commonly used by many to keep physically clean.

Add ¼ cup bicarbonate of soda (baking soda) to the regular bath water. It will not only make your bathing easier, but over a period of regular use, it may help rid you of body odor, lighten your aura, and add to your general well-being.

This simple bath has produced more testimonials than any other. People have reported an assortment of cures that were not the original reason for taking the bath! These cures include such things as the healing of hemorrhoids, thickening of hair, cessation of nightmares. As I feel these cures occur only through the spiritual evolution of the individual, I cannot recommend them as a healing. To my mind, any benefit aside from a gradual and general lightening of the individual over a long term is strictly a side benefit. (I must admit that I add baking soda to my tub baths on a regular basis.)

Psychic Tension Bath

This bath also has a reputation for healing. It is made with Epsom salts. Mix:

   ¼ cup Epsom salt
   1 cup bicarbonate of soda (baking soda)
   1 tablespoon salt (use either sea or table salt)

This bath should be taken without soap. Simply soak in it for ten to twenty minutes. It helps release both physical and psychic tension, as well as promoting a general physical healing of the body.

Herbal Baths

Herb baths are made by making tea of the herb, and using the tea in the bath. Generally, you take 1 teaspoon of the herb desired and pour a cup of boiling water over it. Steep until the tea cools to room temperature. Then strain out the herb. One cup of tea to half a tub of water is sufficient. Proceed with the bath using the directions previously discussed (see section about Ritual Baths).

Basil

Regular cooking basil, either fresh or dried, may be used in a bath. It has a protective and cleansing effect, removing negativity and protecting against the accumulation of further negative influences. It has a powerful effect on certain people. It should be used when you feel threatened by others, victimized or soiled by contact with negative or overly-aggressive people. When using this bath, pray for spiritual cleanliness and protection. Stay in the bath for 6 minutes and immerse yourself 4 times.

Cinnamon

Regular cooking cinnamon, in powder or broken stick form, may be used to help resolve problems at work or at home. Pour a cup of boiling water over a teaspoon of powder or one or two sticks and let it steep as you would any other herb. It helps stop quarrels or dissension. It can also be used to improve your income. Stay in the tub for 5 minutes and immerse yourself 4 times. Pray for protection and calmness, or for the improvement of your finances.

The Money Cinnamon Bath

Add 1 cup of cinnamon tea to 4 cups of parsley tea. Divide the mixture into 5 equal parts. Take 5 baths on 5 consecutive days. Pray for financial improvement. Don't be specific about the source of your financial improvement, but let the universe provide the answers. Stay in the tub for 6 to 8 minutes and immerse yourself 5 times.

Cinnamon Conception Bath

A cinnamon bath has been used to assist couples who wish to conceive and bear a child. Each partner should take a cinnamon bath. The bath is made simply with a cup of cinnamon tea added to the bath water.

Each partner should take a separate bath, each using a separate cup of tea. Both partners should take this bath consecutively—i.e., on the same day or night, one right after the other. Stay in the bath for 6 to 8 minutes. Immerse yourself 7 times. As soon as both are finished taking the baths, intercourse should take place. The prayer said in the tub should be for a healthy pregnancy and a safe delivery.

Coffee

A coffee bath will assist in revitalizing an individual in the process of recovery from any physical illness. It may be used while the individual is still in a weakened condition, but recovering. This bath is an exception to most spiritual baths, in that if it is the *first* tub bath taken after the onset of an illness, the coffee can be added to a soap and water cleaning bath.

All you do is add 3 to 6 cups of strong coffee to the bath water and soak in it for at least 10 to 15 minutes. Please respect your bath, and make the coffee from scratch. This is not the time for any instant brand!

Coffee Hard Work Bath

The coffee bath, made by using 3 to 6 cups of strong coffee added to the bath water is also useful as a soaking bath following an extra-hard work week. It has the effect of assisting the natural vitality. As a *hard work bath* it should only be taken on a Saturday morning. Soak for at least 8 to 10 minutes.

Hyssop

Hyssop is the "cleansing herb" of Judaism. It is mentioned in the Bible (see Psalms 51:7). Hyssop forms a part of Jewish ritual (see Exodus 12:22). It is used similarly in Christian practice (see John 19:29 and Hebrews 9:19). It can be used in a *mickva* tub bath by any sincere Jewish person who wants to become spiritually cleansed. For Christians, it has both a cleansing and purifying effect.

For this bath, mix a cup of the tea in a half tub of water. Stay in the water 6 to 8 minutes and immerse yourself 5 times. The prayer should include a request for spiritual cleansing and spiritual enlightenment.

Nutmeg

Powdered nutmeg used in a cup of tea for a bath makes people more open to listening to you. It is said to increase one's luck, but what it really does is remove those negative thoughts which act to make you unlucky. The powdered nutmeg may be strained away from the tea by using a coffee filter. This is the kind of bath that helps one during times of personal stress such as that engendered when approaching an important interview, or when one is apprehensive about the result of an upcoming important conversation. It can be used when you are apprehensive about such important conversations as discussing your "druthers" with a mate who has been heretofore unresponsive to your needs. It can be used when discussing family matters with relatives who you feel will be unresponsive. It has a host of uses. Obviously, you will need to use it because you have been unsure about expressing your personality. As you take other baths listed here, and develop more self-confidence, you won't have as much need for this kind of a bath.

Use a cup of the tea in your bath. Stay in the tub for 8 to 10 minutes and immerse yourself 6 to 8 times. You may wish to pray for the resolve and strength you need to obtain what you desire.

Parsley

This bath can be used for economic improvement. When parsley is combined with cinnamon it becomes quite powerful. (See instructions under Cinnamon.) When using fresh parsley, you should use the whole bunch you buy in the store. It can be cooked or simmered in a pot with a quart of water for 15 to 20 minutes. Dried parsley can be used as well, and might work better when you combine it with cinnamon.

Parsley and Honey

This bath can be used by a woman who finds that life has no joy for her. For a man, this bath helps alleviate a condition that causes him to be overly harsh on himself. It is made by adding a tablespoon of honey to a cup of parsley tea. This mixture is added to the bath water. Stay in the tub for 6 to 8 minutes and immerse yourself 5 times. Because this bath is intended to correct these unpleasant spiritual conditions, the individual should pray that his or her life be sweetened. Some readers may feel that this is an unnecessary spiritual bath, but it isn't. Many people know little joy in life, and until that joy is discovered, it is difficult to proceed very far on any spiritual path.

Rue

Like hyssop, rue is not a culinary herb, but is of sufficient importance to include here. Rue is the "Herb of Grace" in the Christian religion. A bath made of rue should be effective in eliminating religious confusion. It helps to establish an individual on the proper path in the Christian religion.

This bath should not be overlooked either, as many young people today are attempting to give up their heritage. We are born into a particular religion for a particular reason. Most lay people in any religious order are unaware of the philosophy or ritual of the family religion. Until the symbolism of the religion is understood, we cannot really leave what is our heritage, for it comes back to get us. This bath can be used to enlighten one as to the direction that needs to be pursued.

Use 1 cup of tea in a half tub of water. Stay in the water 8 minutes and immerse yourself 5 times. Pray for clarity about the spiritual path as well as for spiritual cleansing.

Rue and Hyssop

Baths of either herb (not mixed) are particularly recommended to those who have considered leaving the religion into which they were born. One chooses to be born into a particular religion for a reason. To leave that religion before one has learned the lessons of it, or to remain after the lessons have been mastered is foolish. If one is ready to leave a religious practice, he should depart cleanly, without any recriminations. He should not hold ill feelings or bitterness toward the religion or those who preach or practice it. Until this state of consciousness is attained, something is yet to be learned from the religion. If one is not finished with the religious practice, either rue or hyssop baths will give confidence while remaining with it. Conversion is always a serious question, and those who wish to convert should spend a great deal of time in self-examination before they do so. These baths will assist those whose path is within a particular religious framework.

When a person wishes to leave the religion of his childhood, he often thinks he is more free of it than he really is. We see the strength of religious belief and training when the individual is under tremendous stress. When illness strikes, people return to God. When a convert experiences the guilt and grief of death in the family, the early religious training comes back. It is not uncommon for a Southern Baptist to become a Buddhist while living in sophisticated New York City only to say "she's safe in the arms of Jesus," when his wife dies unexpectedly. We seldom know how unfree we are. In order to work at establishing our freedom, the baths mentioned above can be of great assistance.

Sage

When ordinary cooking sage (either powered or leaf) is used as a bath, it has the unique quality of assisting one in gaining true wisdom. Someone who wishes to attain this state of being should take this bath every Thursday morning at sunrise, reviewing the events of the week and any reactions to those events. Nine immersions and at least 9 minutes in the tub are the usual practice. I have found this bath assists the individual by aiding in the destruction of illusion—which is what wisdom is all about!

Household Baths

Obviously there are many other herbs that can be used in baths. It is not a good idea to experiment with them as you don't know what you will be creating. Two common kitchen herbs mixed together can aid in bringing destruction upon yourself. So leave the experiments alone. We laugh when we hear the phrase, "Don't fool with Mother Nature" but in this case it is true.

There are a number of baths that can be made at home from common household products that can help change certain conditions that occur in daily life.

Baking Soda Baths

Before abortion was legalized, it was seldom used as a means of ending an unwanted pregnancy. Girls from good families went to the family doctor; poor girls went to the curador or healer; respectable middle class girls were butchered by incompetent back alley abortionists. Years ago, abortion was handled at home, and unwanted or accidental pregnancies were ended by using herbs such as rue, pennyroyal, or the common household remedy we know as Epsom salts. Today, abortion has become a controversial issue that we are not concerned with here, but we are concerned with countering the aftereffects of abortion regardless of how the abortion was performed.

Any kind of abortion (including ones induced by herbs or folk remedies) will always effect the spiritual grounding and it takes time to alleviate the condition. The effect of an abortion can be countered by taking baths using one pound of baking soda. Take this bath three different times on the first day, then take it once a day for a week. This bath series cannot be started until two weeks after the abortion has taken place. It is a good series of baths to take after a miscarriage as well, for it will have a lightening effect on the individual. At the end of the series take a basil bath.

Baths designed to promote healing do so by cleaning away the cause for the difficulty which exists on the spiritual level. For this reason, any spiritual bath may have some physical benefit attached to it. However, because the cleansing occurs on a spiritual level before the physical results become manifest, it will not be readily apparent that healing is occurring. People who use Epsom salts or herbs as a regular means of birth control—or even those people who use legal abortion as a means of birth control—are misusing the privilege. A person who has experienced many abortions may need to pursue a series of baths leading to spiritual grounding.

The Blue Bath

Laundry blueing powder can help revitalize. It is also particularly good in healing aftereffects of sunburn. Use ½ teaspoon of the powder, or one "blueing ball," or a teaspoon of blueing liquid. This should be added to a soaking bath (a full tub) and you should relax in it for 10 to 15 minutes. This bath can be taken on two consecutive days when suffering from extreme tiredness or lassitude following overexposure to the sun. It is also useful taken a day or two after a beer bath if a feeling of low vitality is present.

Indigo is the active ingredient in this bath and is present in blueing. However, the bath has also worked when someone simply used blue food coloring. Blue is what is required.

Carnation Baths

One of the best cleansing baths is made from carnation flowers. The blossoms of seven white carnations should be placed in a half tub of water. Once in the tub, scrub yourself from head to foot with the blossoms. The petals will begin to fall apart. This bath will thoroughly cleanse your aura. It absorbs negative influences and washes them away.

Because the petals fall apart as you wash away the negativity, a strainer of some kind should be placed over the bathtub drain to catch the petals and leaves as the water drains out of the tub. Pick up the petals and leaves and put them in the garbage when you are through with them.

This bath has no time limit. You don't need to immerse yourself as you are washing away the negativity with the flowers. During the time in the tub, you could concentrate on spiritual cleansing and pray for spiritual purification.

Rye Flour Bath

Baths may be made from a number of fairly unusual substances, each of them having their own effect. This is one reason why you should not experiment, as you may do damage to your non-physical body by taking a bath that sounds really neat, but causes an unanticipated reaction.

One of the more interesting baths is one made from rye flour. Sift about a cup of rye flour into the tub as you fill it with water. Once you have sufficient water in the tub, stir the bath to mix the rye flour in thoroughly. Then immerse yourself in the water four or five times as you soak in the tub for at least five to seven minutes.

This bath has the property of relieving and releasing resolved issues from the bather's subconscious mind. By releasing resolved issues, they are less likely to come up in the person's conscious mind to trouble them again.

The discerning person will realize that rye grain must have some connection to the faculty of human mentation. That this is correct may be shown by another connection between rye and human mentation. Ergot, the black mold that infrequently grows on the rye plant, is responsible for causing severe mental difficulties in people who eat foods made from rye flour that has been poisoned with the mold.

Hydrogen Peroxide Bath

Another household bath may be made by adding a bottle of drugstore hydrogen peroxide to a tub of water. It is important that the drugstore variety of 3 percent hydrogen peroxide be used instead of the 30 percent hydrogen peroxide, which is infrequently available in health food stores. Using a stronger solution of hydrogen peroxide will not have the same effect, as it is too strong to use as a bathing solution, even diluted in a tub of water.

The slight amount of excess oxygen that the hydrogen peroxide provides in a bath makes it possible for the person who is bathing to resolve issues of impiety and immorality. This bath releases the thought forms concerning this issue from the person on an unconscious level. It is often worthwhile to take this bath when you feel debilitated, or just "worn out." It may or may not have any real or permanent effect, but it usually provides at least temporary relief from worn and stressed conditions.

Other Household Baths

There is an Indian soap that is available in Indian stores and in some New Age stores. Often called "green soap," the correct name is Chandrika Ayurvedic soap. It is used in the bath just like any other soap. It has the quality of being able to wash away most of the astral detritus that people seem to gather on a daily basis. I highly recommend using this soap, if you are able to find someone who supplies it. I use it myself, purchasing it from a nearby Indian grocery store.

Castile soap is another favorite of the spiritual practitioner. This almost transparent soap has a slightly elevating quality to it. Aside from using it for general cleansing purposes, washing the body with Castile soap in a bath taken with three tablespoons of ground white eggshell in the water will increase the soap's elevating quality and often free a person from obsessive thoughts and negative indoctrination or beliefs.

Love Baths

The most popular baths sold in religious supply stores concern love. We laugh at people who do this, but remember that love is one of the most important feelings in the world. It is so important that we have trouble expressing it, and any block regarding our ability to love or be loved is worth removing. The result is always a happier and nicer person. When we feel good about ourselves, we can advance spiritually in a much healthier manner. We have all seen the religious fanatics, or the so-called spiritual folk who are cold and unfeeling, and they end up being living denials of what they preach.

Yarrow Love Bath

One of the most effective love baths that a person can take is easily made at home. It is made with yarrow leaves. They must be grown locally, or grown on your windowsill or in your garden, because they have to be picked shortly after the New Moon phase has begun. The fresh yarrow leaves should be placed in a clean one-quart mason jar that has a lid. Use about a cup of leaves, cover them with water, close the jar and leave it in the refrigerator for one week. Use the water only (not the leaves) in the bath, and take your bath on a Friday morning, before noon. The leaves should be thrown away and not used again. The effect of this bath makes a subtle announcement to the universe that you are available for a lover.

Stay in the tub for 6 to 8 minutes and immerse yourself 6 times. During the bath pray for a lover who will love you, who is also someone you can love. It might be wise to also look to love someone you like. Be careful about what you ask for because you might get it.

Parsley and Honey

This bath was listed in the section on Parsley. It can be used to attract a lover or to increase finances. When using the bath for a lover, a prayer must be said while bathing in order to achieve the result you want. Stay in the tub 6 to 8 minutes and immerse yourself 6 times.

Nuts

Certain kinds of nuts can be used for baths. The procedure is different than for the herb bath. Nut baths are made by boiling a few nuts in an iron pot for a fairly long period of time. Fresh water must be added occasionally, and when the cooking is completed, you should have about a quart of the mixture to add to the tub bath.

Only an iron pot is used for nut baths. Pots made from other metals influence the intention of the bath in an adverse manner. Neither nut nor herb baths should be made in aluminum containers. Aluminum is not a natural metal, but is made of aluminum oxide ore. The nature of aluminum places it out of harmony with the nature of the plants and nuts you wish to use. Generally speaking, it is better to use iron or stainless steel cookware. This is an important point to observe when making baths.

Walnut Bath

The walnut bath is a cleansing bath. It has the specific property of assisting in the breaking off of a relationship or any contact with another person. These ties are severed through the use of the walnut bath. Be sure that you want to end the relationship before you fool around with this bath, for there is no going back when you have done this. The "cutting off" may only be done once in this manner. Many people say they want to end something, only to wish to return to a bad relationship because nothing else has come along. Using a bath has its responsibilities.

Boil six walnuts (unshelled) in an iron pot for about three hours, adding water as required. You can start with a quart of water but more will have to be added in the cooking process. You will end up with a hot black liquid that can be used as a bath after it cools. Mix the liquid in a half tub of water and bathe for 8 minutes, immersing yourself 7 times. Pray to end the connection or involvement.

Almond Bath

If you wish to become a more loving person you might try to open up your loving nature through the use of an almond bath. Opening up the loving nature is being able to give and receive loving. Loving, in this case, should not be confused with sex, for that can be done without love.

Boil six whole almonds (unshelled) in an iron pot, just as you did for the walnut bath. Bathe for 6 minutes, taking an immersion every minute for a total of 6 immersions. You must pray that you can open yourself to love, and pray to increase your ability to love others, even those who hate you.

Hazelnut Bath

Hazelnuts are for wisdom, and this bath will give you a bit of mental stimulation. More important, it will keep your mental body clean for a few days. This bath might be used under the following kinds of circumstances: mental depression, unfocused thoughts, lack of mental clarity, unusual difficulty with speech or communication.

The bath is made the same way as the walnut bath. Use nine whole (unshelled) hazelnuts. Bathe for 9 minutes and immerse yourself 9 times. As you might gather, nine is the number of wisdom. Pray for increased mental clarity or an end of the specific mental condition.

Pecan Bath

Pecans will occasionally help some people with personal finances. Don't use them in a bath if you eat a lot of pecans, or if you consider pecans a delicacy. This is a tricky bath and while it is good for some people it can have negative results on others. If you don't eat pecans, and wish to try this bath, it is made the same way as the other baths except that you must use a *copper* pot.

Copper is considered the metal belonging to Venus and she rules beauty and comfort. Wealth is the condition that helps us live in beautiful surroundings and in considerable comfort, so we use copper here. Cook 6 pecans for several hours. Bathe for 9 minutes and immerse yourself 1 times. Pray for increased personal wealth, income or a change in your financial condition. Don't be specific about the source of the funds as the universe will probably have a better solution than you will.

Cleansing with Water 5

Introduction

We have gained some familiarity with water and how it can be used in spiritual baths. Now consider water in its natural state, and see how it may be used for spiritual cleansing. Water has a number of uses and when it is combined with herbs or other ingredients, it can be very useful for cleansing. Water is, after all, the largest single constituent in life on earth!

In several religious traditions,* God told King Solomon he created the sea to absorb and hold every evil thing. For this reason the noble and learned monarch deposited the flasks and bottles containing ten thousand evil spirits into the sea. He had contained the evil spirits to relieve the sufferings of humanity. Along the shores of the Eastern Mediterranean many stories are still told about fishermen bringing up one of the ancient bottles. The men have remarkable adventures with the genii-spirits that are released from the bottles when they are opened.

Sea water is powerful for absorbing and removing negative influences. Fresh water can be used for this purpose as well. All fresh water

---

* Believe it or not, Judaism and Christianity share King Solomon with those of Islamic, Mandian (a sect formed by John the Baptist), the Gnostic Christians, and both the Nestorian Christian and Nestorian Chinese sects.

falls upon the earth and is simply "passing through" on its way to the oceans. When fresh water is used in cleansing, it is simply necessary to command it (through prayer) to take the negativity it is removing to the ocean. If there is a difference and a similarity in the effects of fresh and sea water, we might inquire as to whether there is a difference between the effects of other types of water. Those who have devoted time to opening the intuitive faculty assure us that there is a difference. They say that each kind of water has its own particular function, and thus its own use in the universal scheme of things. We will discuss some of the various kinds of water and see just how they can be used for spiritual cleansing.

Holy Water

Holy water is consecrated by an ordained Roman Catholic or Episcopal priest in the following manner. Ordinary table salt is cleansed of any possible negative influences through a prayer of exorcism, and then blessed by asking God's blessing on it. It thus becomes consecrated salt. Regular tap water is exorcised in a similar manner, consecrated salt is added to it, and the salt-water mixture is blessed and prayed over. Once the water is so consecrated, it should be treated with respect.

Some people wish to consecrate their own holy water, but I do not advise this. In those cases where holy water is not available, or the local clergy has no belief in its efficacy, self-consecration of water may be done. It must be undertaken only by someone who has a strong belief in the validity of the act of consecration and a dedication to the Christian religious practice as exemplified by Jesus Christ. A ritual for the purpose of the consecration is given in Dion Fortune's book *Psychic Self Defense* published by Samuel Weiser, Inc., York Beach, Maine.

Most Protestant churches don't believe in holy water or its effects. For this reason, Protestant believers are not able to perform a valid consecration. Until a practicing Christian is perfectly convinced that he has the moral right to consecrate water he is better off obtaining holy water from a local Roman Catholic church. Unfortunately, some Roman Catholic and Episcopal priests do not believe in the changing of the non-physical properties of water by consecration either.

Holy water has the virtue of God placed within it, to the extent that the priest is able to consecrate it. When it is sprinkled throughout a house it will lighten the vibration there, making it a more pleasant place to live. Used in a bath it has the effect of lightening the vibration of the sincere believer. It may also be used in a daily blessing ritual, in which one blesses himself with holy water. This places the individual in a particular state of mind and makes it easier to cope with the events of the day.

A small vial of holy water can be carried and used as a charm to ward off negative influences. Put it in your pocket or purse. During the day, pray and bless yourself with water from the vial whenever you wish. Holy water can also be sprinkled over food to impart divine blessing on it.

Sea Water

Sea water is the generic term for the salt water of the world's oceans. It is available only at the seashore, and is rarely shipped across the country. Occasionally sea water can be found in half-gallon bottles at health food stores, but this is more rare than common.

Going to the seashore to collect sea water is a worthwhile thing to do. It is a good idea to get your sea water on an incoming tide rather than at low tide, as it is more pure when the tide is coming in. In mild weather, one can bathe in the ocean at the same time, and gain the benefits that ocean bathing provides. Swimming in the ocean has a cleansing effect all its own, and those who live near enough to the ocean to take advantage of this should do so.

As we have mentioned before, sea water has the virtue of absorbing negative vibrations. It may be used for this purpose by anyone who wishes to clean anything of negativity. Because it has this specific purpose, it can be used in a bath, as a component of a floor wash, or to soak something clean in. Even before King Solomon deposited the ten thousand evil spirits into the sea, the sea was the depository for all kinds of effects which have acquired negative energies and are to be disposed of.

Sea water can be used many ways. You can mop the walls of your home with it. To do this, take a sponge mop and dip it in sea water. Squeeze it out so that the mop is only damp. Then go over the walls and remove the negative vibrations. You'll notice how the room lightens up. Rugs can be mopped the same way. Wooden furniture can be wiped down with a damp sponge. This is especially good when you buy used furniture, as it cleans off all the "vibrations" left by the previous owners and their problems. You can also add about a cup of sea water to a three-gallon mop bucket of regular water to provide an excellent solution for mopping down or washing. This mixture can be used to damp mop floors when you wish to remove nasty attitudes or the memories and traces of unwanted guests. This mopping solution is an excellent cleanser when people have come to visit and have been in a confused state. Even those we love become confused, upset, irritable or depressed from time to time. But why put up with their leftover vibrations?

Sea water can be used as an ingredient in other preparations in order to help work out the negativity more easily. For example, when someone wishes to take a spiritual bath to cleanse himself of a particular habit or state of mind, adding sea water to the bath helps to eliminate some of the resistance to the bath. Even though we want to cure our own problems, we often find ourselves resisting the cure. Sea water helps strengthen the force used in the cleansing bath so it can do its job better. Perfumes and other substances which are used for certain effects can also be strengthened by adding a dash of sea water. (Usually a drop or so is enough.)

River Water

The waters of the seas and oceans are salty. Rivers, streams, and lakes are fresh water. While the seas are unto themselves, fresh waters are always found connected to the land that holds them in its embrace and defines their boundaries. The only way the fresh waters can escape the embrace of the land is to lose themselves in the ocean.

River water is a common source of drinking water. Even after it passes through a filtration and purification plant, it is still river water. If you live in an area that obtains its drinking water from a river, you might consider that your tap is a continuous supply. River water has the virtue of continuous flow power because of the river from which it came. This power can be used to make negative manifestations with a person (or a building) flow out of that person (or place). It will then carry this negative energy to the sea where it will be absorbed and in time transmuted. The prayer over the water at the time it is used is what effectively tells the water what to do in this respect.

Bathing in the Ocean or in Rivers

Going to the seashore and bathing in the ocean often provides a very cleansing and refreshing experience for many people. Whenever possible, totally immersing yourself in the ocean water, along with a sincere prayer for spiritual cleansing, will have as good an effect for a person as a more formal spiritual cleansing by a spiritual practitioner.

Those of us who live in New York City have been spoiled by the ease of access we have to the Atlantic Ocean at Coney Island. For us it is but a short trip on the subway. We forget that many people do not live anywhere near the ocean. For these people, ocean bathing is a major event.

Many times people find it impossible to go to the seashore to take a cleansing bath. In this case, it is possible to obtain about the same effect by bathing in a river. Once again, a sincere prayer for spiritual cleansing should be made, as well as totally immersing yourself in the flowing river water.

If you are fortunate enough to live close to either the ocean or the river, I recommend that you bathe in the water at least annually. It will certainly never harm you, as you need not go far out into the water to bathe. The bath will probably be of great benefit in insuring that you have at least an annual cleansing of whatever the waters will remove.

Lake Water

Lake water is fresh water in its most stable form. It doesn't flow like river water, although even the smallest lakes are subject to the same tidal influences as the oceans.

The lake is the product of the rivers that flow into it. Lakes which are spring fed, either because the spring feeds a creek which runs into the lake, or because a spring exists under the lake, are still lakes. The lake is a receptive and holding power and lake water has the retentive virtue found in sea water. It also has the urge to join itself to the ocean like the river waters. Lake water doesn't work nearly as well as river or sea water when used in a ritual. When used to remove negativity it has too much of a retentive faculty.

Waterfalls

Waterfalls have a vibration of power. As waterfalls are connected with rivers, the power that they have is connected with the power of the river from whence they come. The water of waterfalls may be used as an additional power ingredient in spells, where it usually acts as a magical expediter.

In some cases, the water taken from a waterfall is used in a bath, usually to add power to the bath. An example might be in a money bath, to try and make the incoming money appear more promptly. It might be regarded as having a hastening action in such baths.

Stagnant Water

Stagnant water is water that has stopped flowing. Often it has accumulated biological residue that had begun to decompose. The odor of the decomposing water is what gives it the alternative name of stink water. Such water, while it has an infrequent use in magic, is never used in spiritual cleansing.

Spring Water

Spring water has the virtue of penetrability. It has "sought the light" by its upward quest from underground. Since spring water is available in supermarkets, it is excellent to use in any bath if you desire to promote spiritual elevation. Of all the waters, spring water has the most masculine vibration, because of its penetrative virtue.

Distilled Water

Distilled (or de-ionized) water has no "life" in it. Because it has no specific vibration, it should be avoided for any form of spiritual work. The best way to use distilled water is in automobile batteries and steam irons. Keep it out of your spiritual baths.

Rain Water

Rain water is difficult to use as it has variable vibrations. It should not be used for any spiritual work except by those who have been specifically told to use it by a spiritual practitioner. Once rain water falls into a lake, river, or ocean, it accepts the vibration of the larger body and becomes simply water, no longer rain water.

Water and Herb Cleansing Sprinkles

Now that we have reviewed the different types of water let's look at the ways we can use them to improve ourselves. We have already mentioned sprinkling a home with holy water as a means of driving out spiritually negative forces. There are a number of other house cleaning sprinkles which can be made at home and used when required.

Water for sprinkling a house should be either spring or river water. As bottled spring water is available in most supermarkets, it is a good choice to use. Any of the herbs mentioned previously can be used to make a sprinkle. Place about a cup of the *fresh* herb in a quart mason jar. Add 2 cups of spring water and cover the container. Leave it in the refrigerator for about a week. Then use it to sprinkle the floors and walls of the house, or whatever else you wish to cleanse. The herbs have the following effects when used as a sprinkle in this way:

Basil: Cleans and adds a vibration which gives protection against negative forces.

Hyssop: Purifies and cleanses the vibrations, makes a place spiritually calm.

Mint: Adds a mentally stimulating vibration, good for a house which is for sale.

Parsley: Calms and protects a place, adds a vibration which is better for the woman of the house than the man.

Rue: Spiritualizing, and calming vibration. Can add "grace" to a house. If prayed over before sprinkling it can be used for protection.

Sage: Adds to the resolution of problems, in that it increases the mental clarity of the vibration in the place.

Yarrow: Adds a definite vibration which increases the human love present in the place where it is sprinkled.

These herbs can usually be found fresh, and they must be used fresh as a sprinkle. Do not experiment with herbs, for a sprinkle sets up a different vibration than a bath. If you found an herbal bath pleasant, don't think that you will enjoy living where the same herb has been used as a sprinkle.

For those who have never sprinkled a house: do it this way. Take the lid off your jar of liquid and dip your hand in the water. Flick it toward the walls and the floor. When it is dry, dip it again. While you sprinkle the house, pray that the spiritual forces do what you wish done (according to the herb you have chosen). Women who used to sprinkle clothes before ironing will know how to do this. Or remember how you used to sprinkle a few drops of water on those dry sun bathers at the beach. It's really easy. You don't have to drown your house or even get it waterstained.

Special Water Baths

Specialized waters can be used as a bath as well. You can use the spiritually elevating virtues of spring water to increase the active spirituality. This can be accomplished by adding spring water to your bath.

Bring a clean bowl into the bathroom. Fill the tub half full of water and add 4 to 8 gallons of spring water to it. Add the blossoms of

8 or 9 white roses. After entering the tub, immerse yourself completely right away. Then scrub your entire body from the feet to the head using the rose blossoms. Start with your feet and work up. When the scrubbing is complete, stand in the tub and pour 4 bowls full of water over your head. Then leave the tub. Do not immerse again. Needless to say, the entire time in the bath should be devoted to praying for an increase in your spiritual nature.

Spring Water Floor Wash

An excellent floor wash can be made by crushing a dozen white eggshells into a fine powder and adding a gallon of spring water. If this is applied to the floor following a good spiritual cleaning, it will aid in preventing the accumulation of spiritually negative forces. The room should be cleaned thoroughly first to get rid of the dirt, then mopped to promote spiritual cleansing. This solution should be applied as a final rinse.

Cleansing with Eggs 6

Symbolism and Ritual

An egg is a symbol of the potential for life—especially one of growth and development. It represents a pure state, one in which the potential exists for the fully divine life. Birth indicates an entry into the world of matter and the egg symbolism indicates that birth has not yet occurred. Because of this natural symbolism, the egg is one of the most effective agents for absorbing psychic or spiritual negativity. Those forces which are inimical to life (or growth or development) in the world of spirit will turn from the human or animal victims to which they are directed and seek the egg as their prey.

The spiritual function of an egg is different than agents of dissipation, such as vinegar, mothballs, or camphor. The egg absorbs negative energies from the area where it has been placed. It absorbs without thought or question, whether it is in a chickenhouse, a store, or a kitchen, or when it is used specifically to remove negativity by a spiritual practitioner.

If someone prays over an egg, it is able to absorb more of the spiritual negativity from an individual than if the egg is not prayed over. A sincere prayer will help the egg in the removal of negative forces. The prayer includes the object and helps it fulfill its mission in the ritual. In Western civilization, we seldom have the same respect for what we use, as those, for example, who were raised in less sophisticated cultures. The prayer over the egg is similar to the prayer or blessing used in a mass or other religious ceremony. Prayer directs the egg to the work desired by the person who prays over it. The words of the prayer are manifested. Those who work with such things say you must be careful what you ask for, as you may get it.

Spiritual Cleansing

An egg can be used to cleanse oneself of any trace of spiritual negativity resulting from contact with evil or malicious people. Pray over a raw egg for spiritual cleansing and apply the egg to the back of your neck, moving it up and down from the base of the skull to the "lump" at the shoulder blades. The egg should then be broken by throwing it into the toilet. Flush away the remains.

Other areas of the body can be rubbed with an egg to remove spiritual negativity. These are the sternum (the area between the breasts), the base of the spinal column above the pelvic bone, and the genital area. These are the areas of the human body that most frequently attract malefic negative energies.

Emotional Cleansing

Specific cleansings can be done with eggs for particular effects. The sternum treatment is beneficial for conditions when the emotional nature is disturbed. The treatment on the back of the neck is beneficial when another person may be directing negativity toward you. The base of the spinal column is treated to remove negative thoughts directed toward a person's energy, an activity, or even work-related negative situations.

To End a Relationship

The genitals should be rubbed with an egg when you desire to end a sexual relationship. A sexual contact with another person will always result in an astral connection. This connection will remain for about a year with an ever decreasing intensity when the relationship is over in the physical plane. This connection can be absorbed by the egg if you rub the genitals with it for the purpose of þreaking the tie. This ritual is also practiced by some who are engaged in illicit liaisons. The egg ritual reduces the chance of discovery, for the "loyal" partner may sense the out-of-relationship sexual contact.

Eyestrain

Severe eyestrain, or headaches in and around the eyes, whether or not due to Malochia, can often be relieved by placing an egg over each eye and relaxing with the eggs in place for 10 to 20 minutes a day. A folded towel can be used to hold the eggs in place. All eggs used in the removal of spiritual negativity should be broken in the toilet and flushed away.

Physical Pain

Pains in various parts of the body can often be removed through the use of an egg. The individual either relaxes with the egg held in place or rubs the afflicted area with it. This procedure is not always effective for the removal of pain, but when it is, the results are startling. Occasionally the pain of arthritis or bursitis can be removed from the arm sockets or knees. If pain in these areas can be removed, it usually indicates that the problem has a psychic or non-physical cause. A spiritual practitioner should be consulted in these instances.

Protection While Asleep

Should you suspect that someone is trying to influence you while you are asleep, an effective remedy can be put into practice with an egg. Your suspicions may be motivated after having several dreams of the person on consecutive nights, or feeling the presence around you as you prepare for bed, or from an attitude you sense or see when in contact with the person. Should you suspect this influence, it is bound to be of a low level at best, and the use of an egg in the following manner will probably put a permanent end to it.

Wash a whole fresh egg in cold running water. Dry it with a clean towel or napkin and write your name on it with a soft lead pencil. Place this egg in your bedroom at the same height as your head while you sleep. Leave the egg in place for a week, unless it cracks or breaks. At the end of the week break the egg in the toilet and flush it away. If the egg should crack or break before the week is out, discard it in the toilet and replace it with another one. Once the egg has been in place for a week without a crack or a break, you should be past the state of being influenced by this person.

Just as any container has a limited volume dependent on its internal area, so will an egg only accept a limited amount of negative energy. When the egg attempts to accept more energy than it is capable of receiving, it may crack or break. At this point the egg must be discarded and another used. When someone is forcefully attempting to control you, and you are using the egg ritual, the more likely it is that the egg will break. Fortunately, most negative people cannot muster enough energy to crack an average egg.

Cleansing a Home

Should you find a vacant house that you like, you can cleanse it thoroughly with eggs before you move into it. The eggs will absorb any spiritual negativity which may be present. This provides a more harmonious vibration in the new residence. In addition, it reduces the time it takes to make the new occupant "feel at home." Simply place an egg in every corner of each room of the house, and leave them in place for 7 days. At the end of this period, the eggs should be put in the trash. Leave them whole—don't break or crush them.

Cleansing Your Pets

Eggs can also be used to remove negative spiritual energy from animals. In the Pennsylvania Dutch country, eggs are used to remove "hexes" or curses from cows that go off milk. At least one Wyoming shepherd has used eggs successfully to keep his sheepdog from absorbing negative energy from his work. He rubs the dog with an egg every time he seems to be irritable or mentally distracted, and he feels that the process is particularly beneficial to the dog.

Cleansing the Sick

Another use for the egg is in the sick room. An egg placed in the corners of the invalid's room will often benefit him for he will rest better. The troubled astral state of the sick, aged, or chronically infirm can be removed, or at least eased, by the presence of eggs absorbing the energy of the turmoil. Place the eggs by the four corners of the bed as an additional aid. The eggs must be changed every week. Eggs spoil when not refrigerated and the absorption of spiritual energy is not the only cause of eggs cracking and breaking!

When working with any spiritual force, suspect the obvious. When an egg cracks and smells of hydrogen sulfide (rotten eggs), don't suspect a spiritual cause.

Cleansing with Incense 7

W hile incense can be used to cleanse a place or fumigate a person, the range in effect varies from very mild to exceptionally strong. Some of the stronger kinds of cleansing incense can actually have a detrimental effect upon those who are unskilled in their use. These incenses will not be mentioned here. We will concern ourselves with using incense to safely cleanse spaces and fumigate individuals. These can be very potent aids to maintaining spiritual purity and cleanliness in a home.

Those aspects of the created or manifested universe which have the most variability between incarnated personalities are those which are the most solid in the astral universe. For example, a centimeter is a centimeter to anyone. It is the same whether it is used to measure wood, paper, or metal. A centimeter is a measure, and the measurement is agreed on by many people. Our physical senses of smell and taste afford no such standard of comparison, as they are developed or "cultivated" senses. These senses have only the most crude external referents among most people for there are no metric standards for smell or flavor. Things that smell or taste good to one person may disgust or sicken another.

Each individual develops an ability to subtly discriminate between various flavors and scents to be able to use the socially accepted standards of taste and smell. For the average person, scents have little meaning beyond their being pleasant or unpleasant, for we don't stress them in our culture. In fact, scents are strongly aligned with the astral realms. The senses of sight and touch used to measure the centimeter are easily learned by all people after a brief introduction to the rules. The relationship to scents on an astral level is not so simple, but it can be learned when one appreciates the concept.

The effect of taste and scent have a greater effect on the astral realms than the effect of solidity (mass) has on the physical. In the Bible we read of the burnt offerings Noah made as being "a sweet savour" (Genesis 8:20–21). The odor of incense and the flavor of food offerings are what energize the astral inhabitants. Incense, being odor or fragrance in its pure form, gives energy to the inhabitants of the spiritual regions.

To some extent, we might compare burning incense to sending up a beacon or flare to attract those spiritual forces we wish to call. Each odor appeals to a particular "force," and the force answers the call. Once the forces come to where the incense is burning, they manifest their nature; thus we obtain the effect we wish in the place to which we call them.

When we use incense to clean a place, we are calling those forces of the astral universe which regularly act to remove negative influences. We are simply calling them and asking them to work in a particular area. When we burn incense to improve the vibrations of a place, to give a place a more "spiritual" vibration, we call on those forces which naturally act to improve the spiritual vibrations. Each incense, or blend, is a sort of "telephone number" which is answered according to the sincerity of our request.

If we burn incense with no real purpose, we may find the forces decide we are calling a wrong number—and they will not act in harmony with our desires. In any summoning, the forces will act only in direct proportion to the sincerity and clarity of the prayer extended. To be able to use an incense properly we must first understand these rules.

Until one has gained familiarity with incense, it is really useless to experiment with special incenses made up from an ounce of this and a pinch of that. The effects gained by these mixtures are beyond the range of perception of most people. The delusions that one's mind provides as to their effects only harm the individual's ultimate development. Understanding and appreciating the effects of pure incense will aid the spiritual development of the individual, as well as assist him in making life a bit better.

All spiritual work is primarily a matter of sensitivity, symbolism, and intent. When proper symbolism and intent is utilized, the matter of sensitivity decreases in importance. Intent is really a matter of how sincere you are about what you are trying to do. What are your real intentions in the matter at hand? Those who have proper sensitivity, which is controlled by how much the true intuitive faculty is developed, need add only individualized symbolism and their directed intent. I say individualized symbolism because people who have a developed intuitive faculty may use symbols peculiar to themselves to attain the same ends I speak of here.

How to Burn Incense

Burning a gum incense on charcoal (the most pure way) is not difficult when you know how to do it, but it can present difficulties to the novice. First of all, you don't want to burn down your house— nor do you want burn marks on your furniture. You can take an empty tuna or cat food can and wash it out. This can be inverted on top of an old saucer to provide a safe burning space for the charcoal. Self-igniting charcoal can be purchased from any religious supply or herb store. These charcoals are lit by applying a match to the edge. The charcoal rapidly ignites across the whole surface. Soon the charcoal will turn red with heat and the incense in powder or gum form can be added with a teaspoon. Add only about a quarter teaspoon at a time, allow it to burn out before you add more. When you place the incense on the charcoal you may pray for the effect you desire.

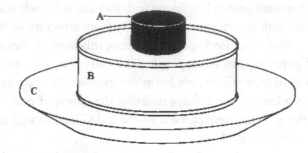

In order to burn incense without marring any furniture, use the charcoal (A) on top of an overturned can (B) placed on a saucer (C).

Cleaning a House

Before you start to clean a house or apartment, or any area, make sure that you have read the beginning of the chapter. The most potent and safe incense for removing any form of "bad vibes" is the so-called dragon's blood. It is a gum resin exuded from a plant found around the Malay Peninsula. It is quite popular in the United States, and can be purchased in many herb and spice stores or occult supply stores around the country. It may occasionally be found in old-fashioned drugstores, in powder form. Usually it is sold as a powder or as a "reed," a stick about an inch in diameter and about six inches long. If you cannot buy the powder you will have to make powder from the reed. This is done by laboriously scraping the reed with a paring knife until it forms enough powder to use. If you have a mortar and pestle you might break off a bit of the reed and grind it down that way. As not much of the powder is required, this is not a particularly difficult process. Dragon's blood has a distinctive reddish color, and is difficult to confuse with other incenses. It has the quality of being both very obnoxious to malefic (evil) spiritual forces and at the same time attracting benefic spiritual forces. It may be said to act as a kind of astral knife, cutting out that which is not wanted.

Before you start to clean a house or apartment, it is important to open all the windows. This lets the malefic forces out, along with the distinctive smell. Once the windows are open, place about ⅛ teaspoon of dragon's blood on a hot charcoal and let it burn until it has given off all its smoke. Wait at least a half an hour before closing the windows. This incense cleansing should be followed with another incense to bring in beneficial vibrations to the newly cleaned place. Frankincense is good for this purpose.

When cleaning a house for the first time, it is advisable to leave the premises for a while. It is not a good idea to have company around when you are doing this kind of work on your newly acquired house or apartment. If you have pets, you may want to be sure they are outside when you are cleaning. This will assure that your pets don't become affected by any negativity. (We all understand that animals are much more sensitive to astral vibrations than people, don't we?) The cleaning will not hurt you, and if you are around for a while it won't have an effect on you, but all housecleaning is best done when you are alone.

To Sweeten the Home

Should you desire to add a lift to your home life, to make life in your home more sweet, you can use this incense after you have cleaned it with dragon's blood. You can use this incense whenever you want to add this lighter vibration. Take ¼ teaspoon of brown sugar and mix in two or three drops of honey with a spoon. The resultant paste is burned on a hot charcoal. Brown sugar is used instead of white sugar only because it seems less acrid when it burns. This does not add a vibration of sexual love, but rather a vibration that leads to a divine love.

Frankincense

When you go to an herb store and buy frankincense you will find you have a translucent amber-colored gum resin. Usually it comes from the inner bark of a short shrubby tree of the family Burseraceae, genus *Boswellia*. It may have been gathered either in Africa, India, or Arabia. It is a material that has been used as an incense since the dawn of recorded history. Frankincense is probably the most frequently used of all incenses, and is certainly the best known. It has the ability to bring a spiritually elevating influence into a place, and for that reason it is the primary constituent of church incenses. Most Catholic religious stores sell a prepared church incense which is 51 percent frankincense, and it is really wonderful for attracting a beneficial influence to a place. You may recall that a chest of frankincense was one of the gifts that the three wise men gave to the infant Christ. Its use is recommended in the Bible, Exodus 30:34 and mentioned in Revelation 18:13. It cannot be too highly recommended, and its safety is undoubted.

Those who wish to gain some control of the spiritual environment should keep a small stock of various kinds of incense on hand, for it can be burned on charcoal as the occasion demands. Only three varieties of gum resin incense are needed: dragon's blood, frankincense, and benzoin.

Sun Moon Incense

Frankincense and camphor, when mixed together in the mortar yield a stiff paste-like material. This material should be stored away for at least six months before it is used as an incense. This allows the incense to "digest" and age. When you burn this incense, use only as much as would be the size of the head of a wooden match. Some people find the smell of this incense absolutely wonderful, while other people do not like it at all.

Benzoin

Benzoin is another gum resin incense. The lumps of benzoin are crystalline, and are easily crushed by hand. It is a much more brittle incense than frankincense, myrrh, or dragon's blood. It is used in church incenses in the Greek Orthodox rite, and more rarely in the Roman Catholic Church. As an incense, benzoin has the ability of directly attracting the higher spiritual forces, and bringing them closer to man. Benzoin may be burned with frankincense to heighten the effects of both, and impart the most positive spiritual vibrations to the place where it is used.

Take four teaspoons of powdered benzoin and mix with six teaspoons of frankincense. When thoroughly mixed add about a quarter teaspoon to a hot charcoal. This incense will promote spiritual clarity, and attract the inhabitants of the higher astral realms to the place where it is burned. It is an excellent incense for blessing a home or fumigating a person.

Myrrh

The three wise men also gave the infant Christ a chest of myrrh. Lumps of the gum resin myrrh are brownish and dull and they have a distinctive odor. Myrrh is also used in most church incense, but for a different reason than frankincense. Myrrh fumes bring the astral realms closer to the earth, opening up the spiritual doorway so that the influences attracted by the frankincense may manifest. In any incense mixture myrrh acts to promote the manifestation of the forces attracted by the other incense blends. By bringing the astral realms closer, it allows "motion" between them. This attribute of myrrh has much to make it a discouraging incense for the novice. It should be used only in conjunction with frankincense, and not burned alone. Unless it is mixed with an elevating incense it is liable to bring negative things to the person using it uncautiously.

Take three teaspoons of powdered frankincense and mix with one teaspoon powdered myrrh. When thoroughly mixed add about a quarter teaspoon to a hot charcoal. This incense will promote a more directed spiritual nature in the place where it is used. It may be used with good results as a meditation incense. It has a relaxed spiritual vibration, reminiscent of the Catholic Church in the days of the Latin Mass.

Copal

Copal is a gum resin incense, which is widely used in Mexico and South America. At one time, it was almost impossible to locate in the United States, but several Mexican grocery stores that carry religious supplies have begun to stock it. If you can find some, try burning a bit of it on charcoal to see if you like the odor.

Copal incense is used to bring people together. It aids in forming friendships, not romantic love trysts. It is good to burn with frankincense, or benzoin, or even with both. If you are working ceremonies or rituals with a group, or even doing group meditations, copal is a good incense to add into your regular incense. It will assist in making your group stronger.

Orange Peel and Copal

Ground dried orange peels, as found in the spice department of the grocery store, mixed with powdered copal, make a nice incense for calming the house. Burn no more often than once every three or four months. As with many other incenses, it is easily overdone.

Incense Cones and Sticks

Cones and sticks of incense can be purchased almost everywhere in the country. They are unquestionably the most simple form of incense to use for they present no difficulty in burning as long as they are burned in incombustible holders. The only problem with prepared incenses is the odor. We don't know who made them, or if the maker knew what he was doing. Indian incense is the best quality prepared incense, and is recommended for general use. It may be used with some confidence that the odor will attract what it is supposed to attract, because the same incense is sold in India to those who use it in their religious devotions. Indian incense marked PUJA DHOOP or prayer incense is the highest quality available in this country.

Sandlewood, the most calming stick incense of all (for most people) has both a spiritual and a soothing vibration.

Jasmine adds a generally calming vibration to a place, and promotes mental calm. It is also an aid to mental clarity, especially when one is emotionally overwrought.

Rose has a spiritual and elevating influence. It can be of some assistance in calming a place where there have been a number of minor disasters (broken dishes, lost papers, etc.), if it is burned along with jasmine. This combination is good to burn in the home to quiet the active vibrations remaining after the children are put to bed.

Pine or other floral incenses should be avoided, unless they are specifically prescribed for a specific condition. Their influences are very dependent on particular odors and intensity, so no general rules can be given.

Household Incense

You can blend your own incenses using ordinary cooking spices to change the vibration of your home. All you do is burn your choice of the household incense remedies listed below to achieve the effect you desire. In some cases these are ordinary household spices blended with some of the gum resins mentioned previously.

Cinnamon Incense

When cinnamon is burned on a charcoal it has a very calming effect. It attracts influences which stimulate the mind. It also seems to discourage aggressive quarrels in the home. It increases the giving nature present in the home when it is burned, so it can be used with good effect before a visit from someone you find negative or miserly.

Allspice Incense

This is good for social gatherings. It attracts an influence that increases congeniality. If you want to create a congenial atmosphere for your friends, burn it on charcoal about an hour before the gathering.

Cinnamon and Allspice Combination

When these spices are blended together in equal amounts and burned on charcoal, they place a smooth and witty vibration in the home. This is a good incense to burn after you have just cleaned out the place. It also adds good feelings to social activities or when you wish to increase the level of communication between people. Although it creates an atmosphere of sociability, it is not a "love spell."

Mace Incense

Mace is made from the covering of the nutmeg and it can be burned on charcoal to increase one's sense of self-discipline. It is a good incense for the study room. It can also be burned when you need to concentrate on a project that needs to be completed.

Alum Incense

Alum has been used medically at times, and it has been a household remedy for many years. It can be obtained in any drugstore. It brings an influence of great solemnity and self-discipline when burned on charcoal. It really should not be burned by itself, as its influence is very heavy. You could combine it with mace to attract vibrations which are conducive to the completion of tasks which are difficult, studying for tests or examinations, etc. For this purpose, combine ¼ teaspoon alum with 3 teaspoons mace.

This incense can be used during the study period if you are a student. Perhaps your children will do their homework better if some is being burned around them during the homework period. If you are interested in concentrating on any subject you wish to learn, this incense would be beneficial.

In addition, this incense, with a teaspoon of frankincense or benzoin added, can be burned when you wish to make a sincere prayer for guidance in finding a good teacher with whom to study spiritual evolution. The sincere student, if ready for this step, will be led to a teacher whose sincerity matches his. Teachers always come in the flesh—the teacher in spirit usually appears to people who are not really ready to learn anything and these teachers are apt to merely glorify the ego of the student. The sincere student will find a teacher who is alive, for this person can help him discover the way for himself.

Salt and Alum Incense

When these two substances are combined and burned on charcoal as an incense, they seem to have little odor. Yet the combination attracts a stable vibration. Burn a teaspoon of ground salt to which an eighth teaspoon of alum has been added. The home will become more stable and it will increase in psychic strength. This incense should be burned only on Sundays during the daylight hours, or it will not have the full effect desired. Ideally it should be burned for the first time during a waxing moon period. (A waxing moon is the period between the new and the full moon. People in the occult seldom wish to use the new moon period until a complete 24-hour period has passed and don't wish to use the waxing moon 24 hours before the full moon is to take place. An astrological calendar or a farmer's almanac will tell you what phase the moon is in.)

This incense and its use illustrates some of the laws of the spiritual world—for the universe has laws as well as the physical world we live in. Using the incense on a waxing moon indicates a desire to make a new beginning. It is burned on a Sunday during daylight because we want to strengthen the spiritual or psychic strength of our home. This strength is symbolized by both the sunlight and the day of the week. When we understand this, the instructions make sense.

Dried Fruit Peelings for Incense

The skin of any fruit can be cut fine and burned on charcoal. This is a pure incense, in that there is nothing present but the fruit peelings. They can be used to affect the spiritual atmosphere of any residence. Fruit incense can help to adjust the vibrations which assist us in living with less wasted energy.

Orange peel, dried with most of the white cut away, will put a calming, but productive, vibration in the home.

Lemon peel has a clarifying vibration, and is often very stimulating to the energy flow in certain people.

Peach skins are good for social occasions when you are concerned about the behavior of guests. It will promote decorum in a subtle way.

Pomegranate skin is an elevating and slightly sensual vibration to most people. Those who find it offensive should not use it again. They should burn a lighter incense, like frankincense, to clear up the pomegranate vibe.

Self-fumigation with Incense

Fumigations of buildings, places of business, and objects of art are really above the level of the average person. Like exorcisms, fumigations should be left to the professional spiritual practitioner. But one form of incense application which should not be personally neglected is the fumigation of yourself. Anyone who wishes to do so is qualified to do it. Just follow the directions below and use the recommended incenses as they are described to acquire the change in vibration that you are looking for. Don't experiment with other incenses, you may create an atmosphere you won't like, and the effect will stay with you for at least twenty-four hours!

Get a straight-backed chair to sit on, and put your incense burner underneath it. Get a sheet (preferably a white bedsheet, but anything of a similar nature will do). Light your charcoal and select an incense from the list below. When the charcoal is hot, put the incense on it and sit on the chair in your underwear with the sheet wrapped around you. It will look as though you were taking a steambath—the sheet should cover everything but your head, and it should drape to the floor around the chair. Be careful not to let the sheet hit the incense burner or the charcoal! Fumigate yourself like this for 10 to 15 minutes.

The incenses for fumigation are listed below. These will suffice for most common problems. Please do not experiment, as you are dealing with your personal vibration!

Allspice: For a more harmonious relationship with others. Very good for difficulties in a marriage, or at work.

Benzoin: To free oneself of spiritual difficulties, when made with a sincere prayer to God for help.

Cinnamon: For protection from others, and calming of oneself. Can also be used with a prayer for a job or a business opportunity.

Coffee: For protection from negative entities. Use fresh (unused) coffee grounds, not instant coffee! Pray for the protection you want. Good to end nightmares.

Frankincense: For cleaning and spiritual growth. A good general fumigation to start out with.

Garlic skins: To remove negative thought forms. Use when you feel discouraged and one thought preys on your mind. (The skins are the outer white part of the garlic bulb that you peel off and throw away when you cook with garlic.)

Honey: A few drops on the charcoal will aid in sweetening one's temperament. (Brown sugar can also be used.)

Tobacco: For physical protection and freedom from an evil influence sent from without. This can also be used with a sincere prayer to rid yourself of the ability to cast the evil eye on others. Break up a cigarette and use the tobacco, or use a pinch of pipe tobacco.

Cleansing Clothing

Sometimes you might feel that an article of clothing you are wearing has "bad vibes." If that is the case, there is an easy way to change the vibration of your clothing. Use frankincense and benzoin incense, and allow the fumes of the incense to pass over the clothing as you pray that it be cleansed of any negativity. Fumigating clothing in this way has been found to be a very effective way of removing all kinds of negativity that it may have gathered over time.

Quieting a House 8

Once someone removes some of the spiritual negativity that affects the general lifestyle, he may wish to clean the home so these forces may be kept away. When this is done, the process of spiritual growth can continue to develop. Spiritually disturbing influences enter for many reasons. They can be removed in a number of ways. The most common spiritual affliction in any residence is due to the process of spiritual upset resulting from family arguments, quarrels and dissension.

Sensitive people may notice that after the first quarrel in a dwelling, the atmosphere changes and is never quite the same again. The original sense of peace and harmony you may have felt when you first moved in the home cannot be restored. Indeed, sometimes the disharmony seems to attract even more disharmonious conditions, so that arguments you thought were settled keep coming up again in various guises to haunt the family. Once the spell of love is broken by disharmony, restoring it is a difficult task.

Dissension attracts its like on a spiritual plane. The emanations of love and harmony yield quickly to the discord of dissension. This process is difficult to understand if one has little sense of spiritual awareness. Those with a sufficiently developed intuitive faculty will recognize this phenomenon easily.

The energy thought forms are loaded with negative emotional energy when we quarrel, and that energy is projected during the course of a family argument. These thought forms can attain a life of their own and even induce further argument and strife. The projected emotional energy of the disharmony feeds them. This condition can only be resolved by cleaning the house of the accumulated negativity. This should be done before retiring for the night following each family argument.

To digress a moment, let me say one more thing about arguments in the home. Many people don't argue much—they have a few words, they disagree about something and then they stop talking to each other. This tension is held in, for both individuals don't like to confront issues that are painful for fear the issue might lead to something else. Perhaps the marriage is unstable and neither partner wants to bring that issue in the open. So the tension stays and stays—but the negative energy thought forms are still attracted to this tension—even when no voices are raised. After many years, a sensitive person can walk into your home and immediately feel the tension and the unhappiness. Sensitives want to leave homes like that quickly. When we discuss cleaning a home spiritually after an argument, this silent argument qualifies for the same treatment as does the one where feelings are readily expressed.

Reducing argument tension can be accomplished during the course of the argument by putting a bowl of water in the room where it is taking place. Another means of reducing the "heat" of an argument is to put ice cubes on the floor, either while the argument is going on or as soon as it's finished. Both rituals make it easier for those living in the home for the ritual helps release the emotional energy resulting from the dissension.

Once the major argument has passed, the whole house should be mopped with a mixture of ½ cup of ammonia and 1 teaspoon table salt in a bucket of mop water. This mixture will assist in the dissipation of the remaining negative thought forms. When the house is mopped, the bowl of water used in the argument room should be emptied and rinsed.

Frequent arguments about the same subject should be termed irresolvable differences. When this occurs, you really need the advice of a professional marriage counselor, or a priest. Rarely is the problem merely right or wrong; in fact there are usually many areas for compromise around disagreements. By consulting a marital relations counselor, differences may yield to a compromise which is beneficial to all concerned. Seeking help from a marriage counselor does not indicate failure. If a relationship is to be resolved, bringing in a third party is a boon, eliminating much unnecessary negativity.

When children are in the home, a surge in psychic activity takes place as the child enters puberty. Puberty signifies a physical phase in which energy levels in the body change tremendously. These changes are necessary as they convert the child into an adult. These energy level changes are accompanied by a variation in the child's psychic patterning. This makes the adolescent child difficult to have around.

Occasionally puberty also brings the opening of the psychic faculty. This is particularly true of young girls during the time immediately preceding and the year or so following the first menstrual period. In the majority of cases, the pressure of social conformity causes the psychic faculty to close down just as promptly after the pubescent child has established a sexual identity. While this faculty is open, however, a great deal of energy is in motion and it doesn't have any real channels in which to flow.

The presence of indirect psychic energy causes an excessive amount of turbulence in the home. This energy will feed any thought forms present and most frequently builds on those that the child generates. The psychic energy can be more intense than the adults are either prepared for or able to deal with. It should be dissipated as quickly as it forms, so the excess energy doesn't place a strain on the family or the marriage.

This energy can be contained and dissipated by giving the child a private room and requiring him or her to sleep with a glass of water at the head of the bed. Mothballs should be placed in the corners of the bedroom. In this way the sleeping child's energy is dissipated as fast as it is generated, and there is a minimum of excess energy available to upset the household.

Just as a house should be physically clean, it should also be kept in a spiritually clean condition. A number of simple actions can be taken to encourage it to remain that way. If these rituals are incorporated in the regular cleaning schedule, the home will respond by being more tranquil for those who live there.

In order to eliminate unwanted emotional energy, add ¼ cup ammonia and 1 teaspoon of sea salt to your regular washing or mopping water. When you do the laundry, add 1 tablespoon of ammonia in either the wash or rinse water. (Note: Do not use ammonia and bleach in the same bucket! They form a noxious and corrosive gas.)

Ammonia is good in the kitchen. A tablespoon of ammonia put down the drain will calm the kitchen and dissolve the grease in the drain as well. This works better than leaving a bowl of ammonia out in the open overnight and flushing it down the drain in the morning. If you intend to clean the oven you might put a bowl of ammonia in and leave it overnight. It will calm the kitchen as it softens the grease deposits on the oven walls.

The same procedure can be followed with the tub and sink drains in the bathroom. This daily procedure can quiet the entire house within a week or so. There is a great deal of truth in "cleanliness is next to godliness." Spiritual cleanliness keeps all forms of negative influences away from those who are spiritually clean. In addition it dissipates those which are in the process of becoming manifest.

For many years a cleaning compound was available which contained creosote oil. Cleaning a place with a compound of creosote oil, ammonia and sea salt will remove the most virulent and negative thought forms. The formula is:

Bad Vibe Floor Wash

    1 oz. creosote oil cleanser
    ¼ cup household ammonia
    1 teaspoon sea salt

Add the ingredients separately to about four gallons of hot water. After you mop the floor to clean it, mop it again with this solution and do not rinse it away. (Do not use the creosote wood preservative for it contains petroleum distillates and it will not produce the effect you want.)

Once you have your house quieted down you should try to keep it that way. There are a few things you can do to make a home a more pleasant place to live. Keep the windows open as much as possible. A well-aired house is much more pleasant to live in, for sunlight and fresh air help dispel negativity.

You might consider having a lot of plants, for windows full of plants add a healthy growing vibration to a place. If you are not particularly interested in growing plants, the next best thing is keeping cut flowers around. White roses absorb negativity from the surroundings. Carnations and roses are excellent to have on hand when you are expecting unknown guests. When you have a party, they will absorb the effluent vibrations. Using flowers in this manner allows you to give a party and still enjoy the vibrations in your home when the guests have gone.

Flowers can be used in many ways when you wish to avoid negative spiritual forces. For example, Indian gurus (and other spiritual leaders) often speak from a stage, which is decorated with cut flowers. The "wall of flowers" forms a protective screen between the speaker and his audience, thus shielding him from the "devoted followers" who are sending him thoughts of greed and desire. Another example that one might think about is the presence of flowers at funerals. This traditional practice could be considered in the light of what we discussed above.

The kind of flowers you use is not as important as the fact that you use them. Color and quantity is not as important as the presence of the flowers. Obviously, the general rule about how many flowers to use would be determined by your space. You can use as many floral arrangements as would look comfortable in your home. The more flowers you use, the greater the effect.

Should you be interested in choosing specific flowers for a particular purpose, the following list might be of interest:

Carnations: have a healing vibration, but are also good to use as decoration. They can be used in the sickroom, or as gifts to those in hospitals. The presence of carnations can be of assistance in the removal of emotional or mental turmoil.

Chrysanthemums: have a nutritive and mother vibration. They are good to have in the home when a new baby arrives. They are the best flowers for the nursery.

Gardenias: have a vibration which promotes harmony between people, especially in partnership or marital situations. The flowers absorb vibrations of marital discord. If you wish to strengthen your relationship, bring gardenias into your home.

Lilies: are good for new beginnings when you are going to try something "one more time." Lily of the Valley *is not* included in this list however. Use the full size lily.

Roses: generally carry a vibration of love. They freely absorb a negative vibration, and are good to have in the home for that purpose alone. The white rose is a symbol of purity and thus absorbs all that is impure. Roses have been found to temper anger in a home.

Sweet Pea: this little flower, when potted and still alive, makes the atmosphere more congenial and social. *Do not use cut sweet peas for this purpose.* Their presence promotes the formation of man-woman relationships.

If you don't want flowers around, or if they are difficult to obtain for some reason, there are other things you can do to maintain the vibration you want in your home. You can maintain a calm atmosphere by thinking of your home as a spiritual fortress. It is the place where you go to retreat from the work-a-day world, a place of peace where no outside dissension is allowed. By building this kind of thought form, you will find that this is in fact what your house becomes and you will enter into a spiritually tranquil phase of your existence.

Quieting the Mind 9

There are times when we may feel mentally overloaded. In some cases, we may feel overcome with grief, sorrow, self-pity, or another strong emotion. Other times, we may just feel that we have too many things to deal with. We may feel that the pressure of all of these things is getting to us, or even that it is wearing us down. While talking things over with someone may be of benefit to us at times like these, we may feel that we just need to clear our head of all of our heavy thoughts and start all over again.

There are many reasons why a person may have a clouded or confused mind. One hundred years ago, the condition of "brain fag" or mental fatigue was well recognized. It was ascribed to doing too much mental work or thinking too much. Those who worked with their minds, unlike those who did physical work, were often found to have this affliction. Sitting quietly in a darkened room and avoiding reading or doing any mental work at all for a time was the usual remedy prescribed for this condition. Because at that time, people were supposed to suppress their emotions, the strong emotional component of this condition of mental stress was not as well recognized then as it is today.

Another condition that causes people to lose full control of their rational minds is hysteria. With hysteria, people lose rational control of themselves due to the presence of a very strong emotion within them. Any strong emotion can completely set aside the rational faculty of the mind. We see this happen when grown people "lose their temper," or when young children "throw a fit." Most of us have experienced this ourselves, as well as seeing it happen in both children and adults.

It is important to understand that what is happening to these people is that they are losing control of their rational faculty. As this loss of rational control, in an otherwise normally healthy person, is always a temporary phenomenon, little can be done at the time it is actually occurring within the afflicted person. Those who become hysterical for some reason, usually work their way out of that state in a relatively short time. In approximately four minutes after first losing control of themselves, they will usually begin to regain some rational control once again. The difficulty with this temporary hysteria is that some people may do permanent physical damage to themselves, or even cause harm to others.

Those few people who have a tendency to display hysterical behavior frequently, usually have an excess of unresolved emotion within themselves. They should seek out the assistance of a psychologist or a psychotherapist to assist them in remedying this often quite distressing condition.

There are ways in which the non-physical component of the human mentation may be cleansed and strengthened. In some cases, these methods should follow a complete spiritual cleansing by a spiritual practitioner. However, as this preferred treatment is not always available, there are several ways in which people may provide "first aid" treatment for themselves. This first aid treatment will usually be found to assist the person in controlling these upsetting emotional problems.

Head Washing

For many centuries, head washings have been associated with initiations into certain religious and spiritual practices. The Christian rite of baptism by total immersion, as practiced by Baptists and others, is an example of a complete body washing at initiation, which naturally includes washing the head. In most Roman Catholic baptisms, the priest will spread some holy water over the head of the infant being baptized. This is a kind of head washing as well.

In many non-Christian religious practices, head washings are given a much more important place in the initiation, as well as in processes of spiritual cleansing. In the African traditional religion, Voudon, the person who performs the initiation is always referred to afterward as "the one who washed my head." Many other religions found around the world also have a place for a head-washing ritual in their initiation ceremony, and frequently in their other rituals for spiritual cleansing.

People may perform two simple head washings for themselves. These are often useful in limiting worrisome thoughts in a person or helping them gain control of the strong emotions that may afflict them from time to time. These two head washings have different effects, but they are often used together, so I will describe both of them as completely as possible. If you decide to use one, or both, please choose to do first the one that most closely fits the mental condition you find yourself in.

Fenugreek Head Washing

Washing the head in a solution of fenugreek tea may frequently relieve brain fatigue and strong emotions such as deep feelings of grief and sorrow. This tea is made by adding a tablespoon of powdered fenugreek to two cups of hot water. The powder is stirred into the water, and the solution is then allowed to cool and reach room temperature. This head wash is then scrubbed into the head, much as a shampoo is applied when washing the hair.

Once the fenugreek tea is scrubbed into the head, it is allowed to sit on the head for at least five or ten minutes. Then it is rinsed off using cool water. The result of this head washing is always a clearing of the person's mentation. The individual is able to think more clearly without being afflicted by the strong emotions previously felt. In addition, this head washing has the advantage of removing nagging and troubling random thoughts generated by these and other emotions.

Unlike some of the other practices suggested in these pages, I recommend that most people use a fenugreek head wash at least twice a year. Our modern life puts its share of stress and strains on us, and most of us do mental rather than physical work today. Because most of us work around people who all have their own emotional problems, it is to our advantage to "clear the decks," so to speak, so that we are not dealing with any problems other than our own. Using a fenugreek head wash twice a year will keep our own mentation clean, reducing negative mental influence from others and allowing us to think more clearly.

Salt Head Washing

When a person just can't seem to "get it all together," or when they have suddenly become "air-headed" and unable to think clearly about anything, they may need to have a salt head washing. This head washing is usually performed in conjunction with a salt rub, or a salt bath. If it is done with a bath, the bath water used is rubbed into the head, often along with an additional handful of salt. Like the fenugreek head washing, the salt head washing is also done by scrubbing the solution into the head, just like a shampoo is used when washing the hair.

This bath and head washing is used for grounding people who feel disconnected, unable to think clearly at all, or who act as if they are "lost in space." Use two pounds of salt to a tub of water and scrub the body thoroughly, as well as vigorously washing the head using an additional handful of salt and the bath water. If only a head washing is desired, add as much salt as can be dissolved in two cups of water and rub this solution thoroughly into the head. Once the person's head has been scrubbed with the saltwater solution, it may be rinsed away.

Feeding the Head

Feeding the head is another ancient practice. Today it is practiced primarily in African traditional religions, but it was once more widespread. There are several different African myths, which give the supposed reasons for feeding the head, and a large number of spells or rituals in various traditional practices that describe how this feeding of the head is to be accomplished. If this work is being done in any of the African traditional religions, which all have specific procedures for this process, the procedure of that traditional religion should be followed.

The procedure for feeding the head, which I have given below, is not taken from any traditional practice of which I have any knowledge. It is a simple generic process, which does have the effect of providing mental stability. As that is always the desired result of feeding the head, I consider it to be a beneficial process for people to use.

Once either of the above head washings has been completed and the person has bathed or showered, removing the head-washing compound from his hair, he should feed his head by using the following procedure.

Either take the milk from a coconut that has an abundance of milk or use an unsweetened coconut cream compound, which may be purchased in Asian food stores. Using the milk taken directly from a coconut is considered by most people to give better results. However, I have found that unsweetened coconut cream is almost as beneficial. It has the advantage of being much thicker and easier to rub into the head than the milk from a coconut. Most people have heads that require feeding so badly that feeding their head with almost anything at all will be of at least some assistance to them in their life.

The process of feeding the head is simplicity itself. The coconut milk or cream is scrubbed into the head, just like the head-washing compound or a shampoo. Once the compound has been worked into the head, the hair may be combed out again. However, unlike a head-washing compound, the coconut compound should be left to dry on the head—preferably, overnight. A scarf or towel may be wrapped around the person's head to insure this. Such protection will also keep the coconut material off the bedding. In the morning, the coconut compound may be rinsed out and the person's hair washed with a shampoo and dried, as it would normally be.

Feeding of the head may be done without using either of the head washings. In fact I have recommended feeding of the head to several people as something that they should do regularly. I generally recommend that it be done at least every three months, as this will insure that the person maintains a reasonably stable mentation.

Feeding the Head with Alcohol

Another method of feeding the head involves using red or white wine instead of coconut milk or cream. The process of feeding the head is accomplished in the same manner. Only the material used to feed the head is different. Some people feel that alcohol provides a better clarifying and strengthening of their mentation than does coconut milk or cream. If this is your experience, you should probably use, or continue to use, wine when you feed your head. Obviously, people who cannot drink alcohol should avoid this practice. Personally, I still prefer using coconut milk.

Please do not think that either of these techniques that promote the health of the human mentation are in any way related to either psychology or psychiatry. These are used to work with the non-physical part of the human mentation, while the arts of psychology and psychiatry work with the more tangible aspects of the human being. Those who are seeing professional counselors should certainly continue to see them. The information given in this chapter will not replace their work in any way. Their area of expertise is quite different from my own.

Selecting a Spiritual Practitioner 10

This book is intended as a first aid manual for spiritual afflictions. First aid has its limits, and while it can be used to alleviate basic problems, more severe ones must be directed to a trained professional. Many difficulties which might be encountered in the psychic realm cannot be solved by the average individual, as these difficulties really involve the work of a specialist.

There are a number of factors which influence the location of an honest and competent spiritual practitioner. Generally speaking, spiritual practitioners are hard to find for several reasons: your own attitude toward spiritual work, the paucity of good practitioners, and the ready availability of fraudulent ones.

First, let's discuss the attitude you may bring with you as a client. Many people have a mental block when even considering the idea of spiritual work. Our culture has instilled in us a belief that all existence is on the material plane, that there is no such thing as "psychic energy." Because most of us have "programmed" ourselves to accept this belief, we refuse to consider seriously that any other form of existence is possible. We can't accept the work or the energy of any spiritual practitioner when we believe in manifestation only on a material or physical level.

Some people may outwardly reject the permeating western cultural belief that all existence occurs on the material plane, but the belief is still held deep within themselves. These people will also reject any real spiritual treatment. It can be difficult for those who outwardly or intellectually think they have rejected childhood beliefs, for the treatment may not work, and they really won't know why.

In order to successfully treat a spiritual condition, the spiritual practitioner must work within the boundaries that the client will accept. When a spiritual practitioner is from another culture, or works within a practice which is unacceptable to the client, the client may not allow himself to accept the help. This means that the spiritual practitioner must personally analyze every client, to the extent of whether or not the client can accept the work. If the client can't accept the help there is no point in the spiritual practitioner making an appointment.

If you call a spiritual practitioner, and for some reason he doesn't wish to see you as a client, don't take the rejection personally. It merely means that he realizes he cannot work with what you need. A rejection of this sort usually means that you should continue your search for a competent worker who can work within your cultural background. You might start your search by looking for someone who works in a way compatible with your own religious tradition—the religious practice of your youth, not a recently acquired one.

People are afraid to work with a spiritual practitioner for many different reasons. For example, some people believe that all spiritual work is limited to praying for the afflicted person. Those who believe this way should seek a priest, minister, or Christian Scientist practitioner to pray for them. They will attain as much from the prayer of their priest or minister as they would from anything a trained spiritual practitioner can do. Christian Scientist practitioners are spiritual practitioners, as are those of the Religious Science Church who "treat" for people. Neither of these groups may like to be classed in this way with Hexenmeisters and Witches, Santeros and Strega, but the cures of Christian Science are just as real as those of the others.

Other people, particularly the Protestant Fundamentalist believers, think that spiritual work involves some kind of compact with the devil. Holding these beliefs makes valid spiritual work for these people an impossibility. Those who believe this should return to the church of their childhood and ask the minister to pray for them.

The percentage of people open to work with a spiritual practitioner is very small. These are the people who will allow the practitioner to diagnose and prescribe for them in accordance with the requirements of their particular case. These people will attain a satisfactory solution to their problems.

The next obstacle in your search for a spiritual practitioner is the problem of finding a good one. There are many fraudulent workers in the field. Palm, card, and tea leaf readers often pretend knowledge they do not have. Some assure the client he has been cursed, and only large sums of cash will free him of it. Usually the client has never been cursed in the first place! An easy way to avoid this type of fraudulent practitioner is to notice how he advertises himself. Store-front signs, flyers on the street corner, and any kind of a "hand-out" advertisement will usually be your clue that this person is not professional. Gypsy fortune-tellers will not be any help in solving a serious problem, or having a serious reading.

The flamboyant personality, the psychic showman is not the kind of worker you need to look for. If you hear of someone who works as a spiritual practitioner, and you hear he is booked months in advance, or that he has a waiting list of the best clients, people in show business and the social register, then you know that this person is not really a spiritual worker. He may be a spiritual practitioner, but a sincere spiritual worker does not let people, even other clients, know who his clients are. If he is "counselor to the stars" other people don't know it, and the stars don't tell.

Don't confuse the spiritual worker with the average psychic. Spiritual workers are psychics, but that is only where they began their studies. Many people have had readings from various psychics and readers. These readers basically cater to the "unwashed public" who don't know much about the occult, and who want to learn some deep dark secret about themselves. Often they only want to find out if the "psychic" can tell them anything. Sometimes these people get good information from the psychic, sometimes they don't. This kind of reader is often harmless, and they can be very useful in their own way. They can help someone break the bonds of the "life is only material" belief, for the psychic may know things that he or she can only know because of knowledge coming from some other plane. Don't discourage your friends from their psychic readings for it may be an interesting experience for them. But this kind of reader is *not* a spiritual practitioner. A spiritual practitioner will not do "psychic readings" for your entertainment.

The sincere spiritual practitioner is not a "psychic investigator." He may be disgustingly prosaic about his work, but he is also calm, efficient, and to the point. He is usually uninterested in your psychic experiences, and will only tell you one of his to prove a point. The person who brags of his accomplishments, or who brags about the fame and social standing of his clients is usually not a valid spiritual practitioner. If he talks about how he suffered to learn, and how eternally grateful you should be to him, you might want to avoid him. If he talks about his power, and how he can use it over other people, he is usually not serving the truth. Anyone who gloats over the spiritual accomplishments or the wonders he has performed is not who you are looking for.

There are a few sign-posts along the way when you search for a sincere spiritual practitioner. It doesn't really matter what practice the individual follows or what format he uses, but there are a few things all spiritual practitioners share in common. By following these sign-posts you may find the needle in the haystack.

1. He doesn't advertise in any way. Clients come by word of mouth recommendation. Occasionally a client may simply walk through the door, not really knowing why he came. The practitioner is not to be found in the yellow pages; he may not be listed in the white pages either. The practitioner may not even have a name on the mailbox or on the door. He maintains a low profile in his neighborhood—although many people may know that he is there.

2. The spiritual practitioner does not live alone. He or she may be married or otherwise mated, or may live with a friend or associate. Spiritual practitioners rarely live alone for they are unable to work effectively without the "earthing force" provided when living with another person who does not do the same work.

3. You will feel completely at home with the spiritual practitioner the first time you meet. In order that the work you need be effective you must have an innate sense of trust in him.

   You must be open and feel comfortable. The trust you feel will be an intuitive and an instinctive one. If this feeling does not take place shortly after or as you meet the practitioner, he won't be able to help you. If the spiritual practitioner senses your hesitancy he will try to put you at ease. However, this will mean that you will have to visit with him several more times before you will be able to accept any work he does.

   Trust is an interesting feeling. We immediately trust certain people—and the trust seems to take place somewhere in our guts. Trust doesn't happen when we use the intellectual mind too much, for then we begin to trust based on an intellectual appraisal of the situation. We are sometimes afraid to admit our "trusts" to ourselves, for we may think that to immediately like or dislike someone intuitively is judging that person. If we listen to our "guts" the intuitive feeling inside ourselves can guide us, and help us know what we need to know, without judging others.

4. The spiritual practitioner will instantly "know" you. He will look at you with a glance that your spirit may feel piercing to the core of your soul. If he has been in practice a number of years, he will have learned to hide this glance—but he also may not. He knows you and will tell you things that strike deep chords within you. Eventually you will learn that

you cannot deceive a spiritual practitioner! It is impossible to lie to one.

5. A sincere spiritual practitioner may not be readily available when you phone. You may get an answering machine when you call. You may speak to someone who takes a message for you, and this person may ask you for your name, birth data, and for some brief description as to why you are calling. You may then be asked to call back in a few days in order to make an appointment. The delay in making appointments usually occurs to avoid the potential client who wants to handle an emergency. When people allow their lives to hang on a thread of time they are indicating that they do not want to take responsibility for their own life. They are really asking that the spiritual practitioner save them from something that they have let build until it becomes an emergency. The practitioner is put into the position of taking responsibility for the person, something that they must refuse to do.

6. Usually spiritual practitioners are very warm and receptive to you. They are also non-judgmental. When you come to visit for the first time, you are shown warmth and friendliness because you are completely accepted by the person who will help you. The practitioner is not cold and arrogant—for you are there to change your consciousness for the better. If you find it difficult to accept warmth, or if you are suspicious of someone who is warm and friendly, this will serve to discourage your further interest in this kind of work. Genuine warmth and sincerity usually go together.

If you are searching for a spiritual practitioner for curiosity's sake, you may be taken for a "rollercoaster ride" which will be good for your soul, but which may leave you a bit shaken. You may be given all kinds of deceptive mystical information that may help you spiritually, but which will eventually expose your motives to yourself. The self-awakening may be rather unpleasant.

In your search there are also three things to beware of; they are not immediately noticeable, but will develop over a period of time while you are working out of your difficulties with the practitioner. They usually indicate a practitioner who has not really developed beyond a certain point. The work may be effective, but the worker's self-development may have flaws. The three things are:

1. Beware of spiritual practitioners who try to "lay a trip" on you. They belong, morally, to the same school as the gypsy fortune-tellers. If they stress overcoming your problems with will power, if they want you to consider yourself a failure, or if they make you feel guilty about anything, they are laying a trip on you, not helping you. Any person who judges you and finds you lacking, who makes you feel guilty, or who places you in fear of the unknown is putting you on some kind of mental trip for their own benefit. They are not helping you. Avoid these moral frauds and keep looking for one who is ethical.

2. Beware of dependency. When a practitioner tries to make another person dependent on him, he is not helping but rather enslaving the client. When a person encourages your dependency he may have negative motivations. This also happens when a worker lays a "holy trip" on you. He makes you feel guilty because he is "holy" and you are not. This does not help. No true spiritual practitioner will do this, as he knows the moral consequences of claiming holiness. False ones will, and frequently do.

3. Beware of immediate acceptance as a student. You are coming for help from a disadvantaged position. Why should anyone want you to join a class until you have your act together? If the request is real, you will get a meaningful explanation. Otherwise be suspicious. This is also true of those who inform you on the first visit that you need to be initiated. Initiation is never properly done to solve a problem in a person's life; it must be done only when someone has assumed responsibility for himself, and grown to the point where initiation can be accepted. Look for another spiritual practitioner in these cases.

Now that you've found a spiritual practitioner, let's take the relationship between you a bit further. When working with someone who can help you rid yourself of any problem you may wish to remove, you can expect to have a relationship which varies with each case.

In fact, each practitioner will have a unique relationship with each client. Usually on your first visit you will discuss the case, and the practitioner will tell you just what he feels has to be done to solve the problem. This may involve anything from his praying over your head, blessing you, recommending a bath for you to take or giving you a prepared bath, giving you some incense to burn, or almost anything similar to the contents of this book.

Should the spiritual practitioner feel that further work may be necessary you will be asked (usually) to purchase an assortment of materials, or obtain them. These can include such things as dirt from a crossroads, flowers, stones from a cemetary, bowls, dishes, cigars, or almost anything.

At your first meeting you will be given a new appointment for the next visit. If you have been told to bring things, you should bring them with you. In some cases you may be asked to bring a friend, preferably the person who referred you to the practitioner. Certain practitioners will not see a client alone, although the discussions are always in private.

Usually, after the second or third visit, the practitioner will give you an appointment a month or more in the future, or will simply suggest that you call him if you continue to have any difficulties. This is an indication that the therapy he feels necessary for your case is over. Your problem will probably have vanished, and the solution is in sight, if not at hand. Unless you know that your spiritual practitioner teaches or accepts clients for long-range therapy, do not be disappointed if he does not ask you to become a student.

Some spiritual practitioners teach and some do not. Some do long range therapy for clients who need it, and others do not. The therapy is not psychology, and usually has no referents to psychology, either in terms or method. In any case the spiritual practitioner will suggest that you study with him only if he feels that it will be of benefit to you. Unless the spiritual practitioner feels that you should be doing the same work he is doing, he will not even suggest training you. It is not very often that one sees one who has the capacity as a client. My best student was almost literally dragged in off the street, and after spending six months telling her she should be helping people, she finally agreed to let me teach her.

If you are having either a short- or long-term relationship with a spiritual practitioner, sometimes the relationship is marred by sexual overtones of some kind. Usually this occurs during the first two or three visits. Should you want to date your spiritual practitioner, or should you feel a sudden urge to have sexual intercourse with this person, you must doubt both the practitioner's motives and your own. You should suppress the desire and examine it later on your own—in private. If the suggestion originates from the practitioner, his or her motives are in question. Why would a helping person want to have a relationship with anyone who needs help? A relationship, by definition, involves a sharing on an equal or almost equal basis. A spiritual practitioner cannot really share anything of himself with a client—except a body! He or she can't share any life experiences or real thoughts or knowledge with you if you are in the process of solving problems. Why isn't your practitioner looking for a relationship with a peer? If the practitioner is really interested in you why not wait until you have your act together, and then introduce the subject verbally?

If the urge to have a sexual relationship with the practitioner originated from you, it's time to question your sincerity. Several things could be operating here. Some people want to drag the person who helps them down to their own level. If the practitioner will have sex with you, then you can't be all bad. At least you are attractive. Some people think that when you seduce a helper you can prove this person wrong. Very insecure people feel that sex is one way to overcome having to face some of the other facets of personality that are not too attractive under close personal scrutiny. The desire to have sex with someone does not always mean you like that person. Sometimes it is used as a means of control. Any desire to have sex with a practitioner should be examined closely, for it is not a mature response.

Before beginning your search for someone who can really help you, it's important to realize that the sincere spiritual practitioner is not working just for your benefit. The true spiritual practitioner is working only for God—and he is primarily concerned with his own spiritual evolution. Your importance as a client is secondary to his primary dedication. Spiritual practitioners help others because they know—and because by helping you they are helping themselves. In other words, they help you as they walk a private path.

Money is another issue here, for often the most dedicated person is not rich. The person dedicated to helping others doesn't charge tremendous amounts of money to do his work—and if you have a problem you can work on clearing up that problem even if you don't have money. Someday you will, and at that time you can help him buy his food and pay his rent or living expenses by donating what you feel the help he gave you was worth to you. In the meantime you should pay him whatever you can afford, no matter how little it is. A truly dedicated practitioner will not refuse to work with any sincere client.

Sometimes a practitioner will quote a fee for work, sometimes not. If a fee is quoted, and you really need to have the work done, you will have the funds to pay him. Some people have lived life in a negative manner, and only by paying a fee are they entitled to the work. Occasionally the practitioner will quote a ridiculous fee because he feels that is the only way you will understand he does not want to work with you. Practitioners tend to refuse work that is requested for the wrong reasons, and they sometimes refuse it in rather peculiar ways.

Locating a spiritual practitioner can be difficult because the real work is unsung. The person on this path has not chosen an easy and lucrative life. For this reason, competent workers in the field are not easily found.

Recommended System of Treatment for General Therapy

1. Read this entire book and make note of what you feel applies to your particular problem.

2. Take the beer bath for Malochia.

3. Quiet your house with ammonia and the salt floor wash. Begin using ammonia in the drains.

4. Begin "sleeping with water" as a nightly ritual.

5. Investigate any particular problem and take remedial baths, use incense, etc.

6. Keep your house quiet by frequent physical housecleaning and floor washings.

7. Begin systematic and regular prayers to your Creator according to your religious beliefs, praying on a daily basis.

Index of Bible Verses Cited

The King James version of the Bible has been used, as that is the version most frequently used in the United States. Chapter and verse numbers of other translations are not the same in all cases. Most of the citations are contextual, as a reading of the context will usually make the meaning of an individual verse more clear.

Old Testament

Genesis 1:6, The division of the waters
Genesis 8:20–21, The sweet savor of burnt offerings
Exodus 12:22, Using hyssop as an aspergilla
Exodus 30:34, Frankincense, one of the altar incenses
Psalm 23, "The Lord is my shepherd"
Psalm 51:7, Purge me with hyssop

The Gospels

Matthew 3:13–4:11, The baptism of Jesus
Matthew 5:43–7:29, Spiritual Instruction

Matthew 5, Prayer as a way of life. 6:6 describes private prayer, and public reward.

Matthew 6:9–13, The Lord's Prayer, "Our Father"

Matthew 18:1–6, Why one should be as a little child

Mark 7:14–23, The evil eye is mentioned as one of the evils that come from within man to defile him.

Mark 11:12–14, The cursing of the fig tree

Mark 11:20–21, The result of the curse

Mark 11:22–26, How to perform magic and work miracles

John 19:29, Hyssop on a spurge

Other New Testament References

Hebrews 9:19, Moses mentioned purging with blood

Revelation 18:13, Frankincense and cinnamon mentioned

Index

About the Author

Draja Mickaharic has been practicing magic for more than forty-five years. He is the author of *True Magic* and *Practice of Magic*. He lives in Philadelphia.

Also in Weiser Classics

The Alchemist's Handbook: A Practical Manual,
by Frater Albertus, with a new foreword by Robert Allen Bartlett

Predictive Astrology: Tools to Forecast Your Life and Create Your Brightest Future,
by Bernadette Brady, with a new foreword by Theresa Reed

The Druidry Handbook: Spiritual Practice Rooted in the Living Earth,
by John Michael Greer, with a new foreword by Dana O'Driscoll

Futhark: A Handbook of Rune Magic,
by Edred Thorsson, newly revised and updated by the author

The Handbook of Yoruba Religious Concepts,
by Baba Ifa Karade, newly revised and updated by the author

The Herbal Alchemist's Handbook: A Complete Guide to Magickal Herbs and How to Use Them,
by Karen Harrison, with a new foreword by Arin Murphy-Hiscock

Liber Null and Psychonaut: The Practice of Chaos Magic,
by Peter J. Carroll, newly revised and updated by the author, with a new foreword by Ronald Hutton

The Mystical Qabalah,
by Dion Fortune, with a new foreword by Judika Illes
and a new afterword by Stuart R. Harrop

Psychic Self-Defense: The Definitive Manual for Protecting Yourself Against Paranormal Attack,
by Dion Fortune, with a new foreword by Mary K. Greer
and a new afterword by Christian Gilson

Pure Magic: A Complete Course in Spellcasting,
by Judika Illes, with a new introduction by the author
and a new foreword by Mat Auryn

Saturn: A New Look at an Old Devil
by Liz Greene, with a new foreword by Juliana McCarthy

Taking Up the Runes: A Complete Guide to Using Runes in Spells, Rituals, Divination, and Magic,
by Diana L. Paxson, with new material by the author

Yoga Sutras of Patanjali,
by Mukunda Stiles, with a new foreword by Mark Whitwell